Coins for Investment

Coins for Investment

Joseph Edmundson M.C., F.R.N.S.

(writer of the *Daily Telegraph* column 'Collecting Coins')

W. H. ALLEN

LONDON & NEW YORK

A division of Howard & Wyndham Ltd

1972

Printed in Great Britain
by Richard Clay (The Chaucer Press) Ltd,
Bungay, Suffolk
for the publishers
W. H. Allen & Co. Ltd,
Essex Street, London WC2R 3JG
Bound by Richard Clay (The Chaucer Press) Ltd, Bungay, Suffolk
ISBN 0 491 00377 3

Contents

Foreword

IN THIS book I have tried to explain, as far as possible in non-technical language, how a person interested in collecting coins can make at moderate cost a worthwhile and satisfying collection which at the same time should show an increase in capital value, so that the sheer pleasure of collecting becomes allied with an investment for the future.

I have tried to show how to buy (and when necessary how to sell) wisely, and how to take care of a collection so that it does not lose value because of the physical deterioration of the coins.

I have taken most of my examples from the coinage of Great Britain in the last two hundred years, but the examples illustrate certain basic principles which apply wherever you live and whatever coins you collect.

If I have included certain information which is also available in numismatic books of a more general nature, it is because it bears directly on the question of investment. The classifications of a coin's condition are to be found elsewhere, I will readily admit, but I make no apology for including them here, because the condition of a coin bears considerably on its price.

I have endeavoured in these pages to give guidelines rather than answers. The coin market is perhaps more changeable than ever before, and long-term predictions are becoming increasingly difficult. Although I have been able to indicate a number of actual market trends, it is much more important for the reader to grasp the principles that I have described and apply them to the current situation.

At appropriate places in the text I have mentioned reading matter which the collector will find useful as he gets more into this subject. Full details of these and other books and catalogues are listed in the bibliography.

Finally, the prices I have given are taken for the most part from *Seaby's Standard Catalogue*, 1972. I am aware that some of them will be to some extent out of date by the time *Coins for Investment* reaches the bookstalls, but that doesn't really matter; it is the *difference* between prices that counts.

JOSEPH EDMUNDSON
St Agnes
Cornwall

COINS AS AN INVESTMENT

CHAPTER ONE

How The Money Grows

One thing I must make absolutely clear right at the outset. This book is not written for the person who is merely interested in money and not in coins as objects of both art and history, nor is it written for the big-time speculator who has large sums at his disposal and buys coins in bulk purely as merchandise with the aim of making a profit.

It is intended for the already ardent collector of coins, and for anyone interested in taking up coin collecting as a hobby and who wishes to ensure that their collection will increase in value.

There are still many purists in the world of numismatics who raise their hands in horror at the idea of making a profit out of coin collecting, but this is in my opinion quite unreasonable.

No wise and prudent person who does not have great amounts of money at his disposal would normally contemplate buying a non-dispensible item which he knew was certain to depreciate in value. I can see no reason whatsoever why one should not be considered a serious numismatist just because one buys wisely and with ultimate value-appreciation in mind, so long as that is not the overriding consideration in forming one's collection. Indeed, the reasons why a particular coin is attractive to a collector are the same as the reasons why it appreciates in value, so that in buying a coin of beauty and historical interest in good condition the collector is simultaneously acquiring an investment likely to appreciate. However, anyone who buys a coin, not because they particularly want it for their collection but simply because they think it will become more valuable, is an investor or a dealer and not a collector, and this book is not for them.

More conventional methods of saving, such as building societies, life insurance, savings certificates and premium bonds, should not be neglected; think of coins first and foremost as an occupation of interest, buy carefully and wisely, and you will have an investment that can produce a rate of interest, free of tax, far in excess of that from most other methods of saving.

You may feel that as a person of limited means you cannot possibly afford to set aside money to buy coins and at the same time save in other ways as well. The simple answer is that you can: you can invest quite small amounts, as little as £1 a year, and still have quite a large amount of capital after only a few years.

By way of illustration, here are a few outstanding examples of capital appreciation which have been produced by coins from the beginning of this century up to the present time.

In 1901, Edward VII came to the throne; coins were issued for nine years during his reign, from 1902 to 1910.

Suppose that your father or grandfather had put aside in mint or uncirculated condition (and taken care to keep in that state) just *one* coin of each type issued for normal circulation each year. In 1902 he would have collected a crown (the only one issued during the reign) and a halfcrown, florin, shilling, sixpence, threepence, penny, halfpenny and farthing, for a total outlay of 11s. 4¾d. (57p) or just over 2½d. (1p) a week. In the remaining eight years his outlay would have been five shillings a year less, i.e. 6s. 4¾d. (32p) a year or just under 1½d. (½p) a week. This would have represented a total outlay for the whole reign of £3. 2s. 6¾d. (£3·13).

Now let us look at the present (1972) catalogue value of these coins.

Taking the first year of the reign, 1902, even in Extremely Fine (almost uncirculated) condition, the coins are now valued as follows: crown, £32·50; halfcrown, £18·50; florin, £13·50; shilling, £7; sixpence, £5; threepence, £2; penny, £2·25; halfpenny, £2·50; farthing, £1·75. In 68 years an investment of just over 55p has appreciated to £85.

The year 1905 was even better, for the coins which cost a total of only 32p in that year are now catalogued in Extremely Fine condition as follows: halfcrown, £240; florin, £50; shilling, £55; sixpence, £10; threepence, £7; penny, £6; halfpenny, £3; farthing, £2·50. Thus uncirculated coins worth 6s. 4¾d. (32p) in 1905 are valued in 1972 at £373·50.

Taking the reign as a whole the figures are: outlay for the whole reign, £3. 2s. 6¾d. (£3·13); present catalogue value in Extremely Fine condition, £1,382·25.

A more detailed analysis of the reign is very instructive. The chart below shows the present catalogue values of all the normal-issue silver and bronze coins, in Extremely Fine condition, for the nine years concerned.

	2s. 6s.	2s.	1s.	6d.	3d.	1d.	½d.	¼d.
1902	£18·50	£13·50	£7·00	£5·00	£2·00	£2·25	£2·50	£1·75
1903	160·00	40·00	27·50	10·00	2·25	3·50	3·00	2·00
1904	120·00	55·00	20·00	15·00	8·00	7·00	5·00	3·50
1905	240·00	50·00	55·00	10·00	7·00	6·00	3·00	2·50
1906	32·00	17·50	8·00	7·00	6·00	5·00	3·00	2·00
1907	38·00	27·00	10·00	8·00	2·25	3·50	3·00	2·00
1908	55·00	42·50	18·00	10·00	2·00	4·00	3·00	2·00
1909	42·00	35·00	13·00	8·00	2·25	7·00	4·00	1·75
1910	26·00	20·00	7·50	6·00	2·00	3·50	4·00	4·00
TOTALS	729·50	280·50	166·00	79·00	33·75	41·75	30·50	21·50

These returns are so large that it is tempting to suppose that there must be a catch in it somewhere, or to point out that your grandfather *didn't* collect all those coins, and anyway things like that don't happen with more modern coins.

The only catch is that the figures quoted are *catalogue values*, which are the prices a dealer will charge you if you wished to buy the coins, and not those he would pay you if you wished to sell them, which are normally half to two-thirds of catalogue values. Even so, an investment of 22s. 6d. (£1·12½) in halfcrowns which produces between £365 and £480 in sixty years is well worth while. Furthermore, prices approximating to catalogue values can often be obtained at auctions run by reputable firms of specialist coin auctioneers.

Secondly, it is quite untrue that appreciation of the kind I have described does not happen with very modern coins – though it doesn't, of course, happen with all of them.

Here are a few examples of 1972 catalogue prices for coins in Extremely Fine condition. Halfcrown, (1925) £75, (1930) £50; florin, (1925) £60; shilling, (1925) £20; sixpence, (1923) £13, (1952) £14; threepence, (1946) £35, (1949) £50, (1958) £2; penny, (1950) £10, (1951) £8; halfpenny, (1946) £3, (1951) £1·50; farthing, (1935) £1·75, (1956) 60p.

Though some of these coins are not yet growing in value at the same rate per year as some of the Edwardian coins have done, others have already grown even faster. In 60 years, for instance, the 1910 penny has reached a value of approximately £3·50, but the 1950 penny has already reached £10 in only 20 years.

The *annual percentage increase* is very important. Suppose, for example, that in 1956 you had obtained just a pound's worth of uncirculated farthings and kept them in that condition; the present catalogue value of these farthings would be £576, an average annual increase of roughly £36 or 3,600% per year. Again, even though a 1960 English shilling is now catalogued at only 75p, this still represents a growth of around 1,400%, or an approximate average of 140% per year, which is a good interest rate by any standards.

So far I have given only examples of coins which have shown a considerable increase in value (there are many others which will be mentioned later. There are of course far many more coins which have increased relatively very little in value over the years. The Churchill crown of 1965, for instance, can still be obtained through a bank at its face value of 25p (five shillings); in other words, not only has it shown no growth over 7 years, it has really decreased in value, on account of depreciation of the value of money.

In nineteen years the value of the 1953 (Coronation year) crown of Elizabeth II has only increased, in Extremely Fine condition, to £1·00 though the crown issued in 1960, seven years later, is catalogued at £2·50 in the same condition. A florin of 1954 is priced at £10 uncirculated, but one of the following year is valued at only £1·50. Many more examples could be given, but it will already be clear that all coins do not increase in value at the same rate and some show very little appreciation indeed.

Furthermore, if one studies coin values over the years, other interesting facts emerge. For example, the values of some coins remain almost stationary for some time, and even decrease, and then suddenly rise very rapidly indeed.

In Chapter Two the main factors which affect the value of coins will be considered in detail.

What Makes a Coin Valuable?

Two factors are of paramount importance in determining the value to a collector of any coin: its *condition*, and *the interplay of supply and demand*.

Condition

The condition of a coin is the product partly of the way it was made, but mainly the amount of wear that it has subsequently suffered.

In Great Britain, coins are usually classified into the following main grades:

Fleur de Coin (customarily abbreviated to FDC)
Uncirculated (Unc.)
Extremely Fine (EF)
Very Fine (VF)
Fair
Poor

Although I have tried to give in the following pages a working definition of these categories, the distinctions between them are comparatively subtle, and ultimately boil down to questions of judgement and experience. To counteract this, it has in recent years become fashionable to subdivide some of the categories in an attempt to give a more accurate description of the condition of a coin which is perhaps on the borderline between two grades.

Thus, a more detailed grading chart could read:

Uncirculated
{
Brilliant Uncirculated
Uncirculated (Some Lustre)
Uncirculated
}

Extremely Fine	⎧ Almost Uncirculated ⎨ Very Good Extremely Fine ⎩ Extremely Fine
Very Fine	⎧ Almost Extremely Fine ⎨ Very Good Very Fine ⎩ Very Fine
Fine	⎧ Almost Very Fine ⎨ Very Good Fine ⎩ Fine
Fair	⎧ Almost Fine ⎩ Fair
Poor	Poor

It must also be mentioned that American terminology differs slightly, their gradings being FDC, Uncirculated, Extremely Fine, Very Fine, Fine, Very Good and Good. All of this terminology must be considered as arbitrary and relative, as will be seen below; words like *fine* and *good* are not to be used literally – or lightly.

If a coin is described as Extremely Fine (or EF) this means that both sides of the coin are in this condition; sometimes one side is more worn than the other, and then the coin might be described as EF/VF, meaning that the obverse or 'heads' is in Extremely Fine and the reverse or 'tails' in Very Fine condition.

Before considering how the condition of a coin affects its value, it is necessary to be able quite clearly to recognize the essential differences between the grades. For this it is necessary to know the technical terms used to describe any coin.

The Parts of a Coin

Obverse	The 'heads' side, bearing the portrait of the reigning monarch, etc.
Reverse	The 'tails' side of the coin, which often bears a design, such as St George and the Dragon, Britannia or other heraldry.
Design or Type	The portrait, depiction or design occupying the major part of either side of the coin.

Field	The plain, usually polished or shiny part of the coin surrounding the design.
Rim	The raised circumference of the coin.
Border	The raised pattern, usually consisting of teeth or beads, immediately next to the rim.
Edge	Self-explanatory. It can be smooth, as is usual in copper, bronze and brass coins, or 'milled' or 'grained', as in most gold, silver and cupro-nickel coins. On the edges of some coins, particularly crowns or commemorative issues, there can be raised or incused (cut in) words and patterns.
Legend	This consists of the words or lettering on either side of the coin; it is usually, but not always, round the circumference.
Exergue	A panel, usually at the bottom of the reverse, in which the date often (but not always) appears.
Exergue line	The raised line which often divides the exergue from the rest of the coin.

FDC (Fleur de coin). A coin in this condition is completely flawless, showing not the slightest sign of a blemish, scar, scratch, nick or dent even when inspected with a powerful magnifying glass. Very few coins are in this condition, except some proof* coins straight from the Mint. They require extremely careful handling, for even a soft duster could possibly cause a minute scratch on the field. All coins, but especially those in this exceptional condition, should always be held *by the edge only*, and never touched on the face.

* A definition of 'Proof' is given in Chapter Ten, page 53.

Uncirculated. Until a coin goes into circulation it normally suffers very little damage. Being thrown together with the other coins during minting will inevitably cause very slight abrasions and occasional minor scratches, but there will be no signs of wear whatsoever on the high points of the design. It is possible sometimes to obtain new coins straight from your bank which show few, if any, of these minor flaws (cultivate a friendly cashier for this purpose).

Brilliant Uncirculated indicates that the coin still has the full lustre with which it left the Mint. This lustre can be maintained by careful protection, but I cannot emphasize too strongly that once the lustre begins to fade it cannot *and must not* be 'restored' by any form of cleaning or polishing, which will almost automatically result in the coin losing most if not all of its value as a collector's piece.

I deplore the use of the term 'almost uncirculated', by the way; a coin is either uncirculated or it isn't. While it is in transit in bags from the mint to the Bank it can be considered Uncirculated, but once it gets into the hands of customers and begins to be carried in pockets and passes from hand to hand, even if it is only for a short time, it cannot be better than Extremely Fine or Very Good Extremely Fine.

Extremely Fine. Many newcomers to collecting, and even some with a fair amount of experience, tend to over-grade their coins and describe them as being in Extremely Fine condition when in fact they are no better than Very Fine.

An Extremely Fine coin will, on casual inspection, appear to be in Uncirculated condition and will show no visible signs of wear, even on the high points of the design, except when viewed under a ×5 or ×10 magnifying glass.

Very Fine. A coin in this condition will still look in quite first-class condition; indeed many non-collectors anxious to sell such a coin will describe it as Excellent or Nearly Mint, though to an experienced collector or professional numismatist it may be only just Very Fine.

In fact the wear at the main points already described will be quite visible without the need of a magnifying glass and the areas of wear will have been extended slightly. Nevertheless the coin will look in good condition and may well fill a gap in a collection until such time as one in Extremely Fine or Uncirculated condition can be found to replace it.

In some cases, particularly when rare or very rare coins are concerned, the prices of such coins may make it impossible for the ordinary collector to acquire them in better than VF condition; modern coins such as the 1930 halfcrown, 1952 sixpence, 1946 and 1949 threepences and 1950 and 1951 pennies are well worth collecting and purchasing in the Very Fine grade.

Fine. This term, like the American Very Good and Good, is something of a misnomer, for a Fine coin is actually far from fine.

It will have immediately obvious signs of wear on all the high points, and this wear will be considerably more extensive than on an Extremely Fine piece. For instance, those coins of the early years of Elizabeth II and the reign of her father, George VI, which are still in general circulation are rarely in better than Fine condition.

Most of the fine lines in the hair will have disappeared, giving parts of the head a slightly bald appearance; the eyes, lips and main features of the face will be plainly visible, however, and the legend and dates will show little signs of wear and be perfectly readable.

On the florin, the details of the buds below the thistle flower will have practically disappeared, the leeks will be almost if not completely smooth, there will be little visible detail on the shamrock leaves and the hatching on the centre of the Tudor rose will be almost invisible; on coins such as the halfcrown which have heraldic devices containing lions or leopards, the eyes of the animals will have disappeared and their bodies and legs will be quite smooth.

Though many very old coins are well worth saving in this condition (mainly because it is almost impossible to obtain them in better grades) Fine modern coins are generally of little or no value, unless they are extremely rare, and are not considered desirable by serious numismatists.

Fair. Though all the main features of the design will still be visible and the legend and date still be readable, the coin will be exceedingly worn. The coins of the early years of George V and Edward VII, if still in circulation, are rarely if ever in better than Fair condition, and again, unless they are extremely rare they are not worth collecting, and worth no more than their face value.

Poor. A coin in this condition is so worn that unless it is of the very utmost rarity (an Edward VIII brass threepenny piece, for instance, or a 1933 penny) it is of no use whatsoever to a collector. The design will have worn completely smooth, and parts of the legend and even figures of the date may have disappeared.

The occasional 'Bun' penny of Queen Victoria, which until decimalisation was still to be found in one's change, is rarely if ever in better than Poor condition. Such coins are almost invariably worth no more than face value.

Before considering the actual effects of grading on coin prices, which is dealt with in Chapter Three, we must examine the other factor which affects the values of coins – supply and demand.

Supply and Demand

The mechanism by which all markets operate is uniform and quite simple. So long as there is a greater demand for an article than there is a supply of it, other things being equal the price will rise. When supply exceeds demand, the price will fall. This is no less true of the market in rare and fine coins. In fact it is more true of things like coins, stamps or paintings than it is of manufactured articles, whose price is affected by such factors as the need to cover the cost of manufacture. Indeed, considering the number of other factors involved – condition, age, fashion and so on – it is surprising to what extent coins can be seen to conform to the rule.

Over the years the coins of a particular denomination, even those which are in demand by collectors, tend to diminish in number. They get lost or damaged, absorbed into collections – both private and public – are turned into brooches and cuff-links or melted down for their bullion content. To that extent they become rarer and, given that there is some demand for them, increase in value.

Equally, there is an overall tendency for coins' condition to deteriorate. Examples inevitably become damaged or worn by mishandling, and the number of good-quality pieces thereby diminishes so that their value, already augmented by the fact that a better piece is always and by definition more in demand than a worse, increases even more. However the quantity of available examples of a coin may well affect price more than all other influences – even condition.

Many people are under the impression that the older a coin is the more valuable it automatically becomes, but this is not so, as the following examples illustrate.

Halfcrowns of George V

| | | | *Current price* | |
Year	Mintage	F	VF	EF
1911	2,914,573	£1·00	£4·00	£16·50
1912	4,700,789	1·00	5·00	20·00
1913	4,090,169	2·50	8·00	28·00
1914	18,333,003	0·30	1·00	6·00
1915	32,433,065	0·30	0·85	4·00
1916	29,530,020	0·30	0·85	4·00
1917	11,172,052	0·45	1·00	5·50

English Shillings of Elizabeth II

Year	Mintage	EF	UNC
1953	41,942,894	£0·25	£0·65
1954	30,262,032	0·20	0·75
1955	45,259,908	0·20	0·75
1956	44,907,008	0·40	1·25
1957	42,774,217	0·15	0·50
1958	14,392,305	0·75	3·00
1959	19,442,778	0·10	0·50

Scottish Shillings of Elizabeth II

Year	Mintage	EF	UNC
1953	20,663,528	£0·25	£0·65
1954	26,771,735	0·20	0·75
1955	27,950,906	0·20	0·75
1956	42,853,639	0·35	1·00
1957	17,959,988	0·75	3·50
1958	40,822,557	0·10	0·50
1959	1,012,988	1·00	5·00

A study of the above tables shows that, generally speaking, the values of these coins are proportionate to the numbers issued.

It also indicates that above a certain size of mintage, prices tend not to be affected by quantity. For example, in the half-crown table it will be seen that, though in 1914, 1915 and 1916 the numbers were approximately 18, 32 and 29 millions respectively, their catalogue values are identical; this would seem to indicate that a figure of about 15 millions is saturation point for those particular years.

In the shillings table the general trend is again evident, though there are one or two anomalies, particularly in the 'Uncirculated' column. For instance in 1953, with an issue of 20½ million, the Uncirculated value is given as 65p, yet the following year, when the issue was over 6 million more, the value is given as 75p and in 1956, with an issue of nearly 43 million, the Uncirculated value is given as £1·25.

There is a possible explanation for this last figure, for similar apparent anomalies occur at intervals throughout the years.

It can happen that towards the end of a calendar year there remain a number of dies still in usable condition and, as dies are extremely expensive items to produce, a considerable number of coins in excess of requirements for that year are struck, but not issued until the following year; thus statistically they would be counted, not in their date year but in the issue year.

Take a hypothetical example.

Suppose that in 1960 some 30 million examples of a particular coin were struck but only 25 million were issued. The mint figures for 1960 would be 25 million. If in the following year, 1961, the additional 5 million were issued along with, say, 15 million coins dated 1961, the issue figures for 1961 would be 20 million. Thus, though a 20 million issue would indicate a fairly low value for that particular coin, the catalogue value would be higher, for the 1961 price is based on the issue of coins bearing the 1961 date.

Fortunately such cases are the exceptions to the rule, and the general principle that the lower the published mintage figure, the higher the value of the coin concerned, still holds true.

Quite apart from any other interest that a coin may have, sheer rarity can give it substantial value. If only a relatively small number of coins of a certain denomination are issued in any one year, or there exists only a known number of a particular coin, then there will be considerable competition among enthusiastic collectors to acquire it, and some of the more fanatical or wealthy of them will pay a high price for the privilege.

The process can also work in reverse. It sometimes happens, particularly with very old coins, that someone digs up a long-buried hoard of coins of a particular reign or denomination which was previously in very short supply and, literally almost overnight, a scarce coin becomes more common and down falls its value. The same thing may happen if a very large collection is broken up, flooding the market with collectors' pieces.

Rarity can often be produced artificially. For instance, when the decision was made to decimalize our currency, before any government action could take place a number of speculators began to buy large quantities of £5 mint bags of uncirculated coins of various pre-decimal denominations and to store them away in anticipation of their value rising after the changeover.

This hoarding has of course produced what is to some extent an artificial scarcity, and a consequent rise in price of a number of quite recent Elizabeth II coins. Sooner or later, however, as the hoarded coins are released on the market, their values could, and almost certainly will, come down.

To counteract this speculation, the Government took the somewhat unusual step of decreeing that all non-decimal coins from 1967 onwards, whenever minted, should retain the 1967-date, and the Banks were discouraged from supplying coins in bulk to customers. The result of this is that the supply of 1967–dated coins has been artificially increased. This makes it even more unlikely that coins of that date will increase in value to any great extent.

Another factor affecting demand is fashion. A particular piece may enjoy a sudden vogue for any of a hundred reasons. There could be a rumour that the price is about to go up, or a piece of publicity on television or in the newspapers, or just one of those mysterious currents of interest as ephemeral as gossip. When money is scarce, expensive coins may become less fashionable – unless a lot of collectors are using them as a hedge against inflation – and cheaper ones more so. The opposite happens when people have more cash to spend.

Occasionally, and often due to the rise in price of coins which are popular and in short supply, collectors look round for others which are less expensive. This in turn leads to an increased demand for the new coins and up go their values, as happened recently to the coinage of the Irish Republic (Eire).

Two other factors which are often ignored are local scarcity and local saturation.

For instance, one might have a coin for which, under normal circumstances, one would expect a dealer to pay £1; but if he already has a more than sufficient supply of that particular coin his offer will be below the general market level. At the same time another dealer, perhaps only a short distance away, may be short of examples of that coin; and he may be willing to pay even more than £1. The mechanism works equally well in reverse: an overstocked dealer will sell off his surplus at a lower price than one who knows his customers will quickly absorb his stock.

These guidelines should help the reader to spot trends in coin prices and to analyse market movements as they are happening; but they are only guidelines. The collector's own experience and observation, together with what advice he can glean from those more expert than himself, are the essential basis of a good understanding of the market.

CHAPTER THREE

Coin Condition and Coin Value

Remembering that serious coin collectors and professional numismatists almost invariably seek for coins in perfect condition and that at the same time such coins, if not always extremely rare, are far fewer in numbers than those which have blemishes of one kind and another, or show some signs of having been in circulation, it automatically follows that the demand for perfect or near-perfect coins is likely to exceed supply – and therefore their values will always tend to be high.

Conversely, and this particularly applies to coins issued over, say, the last 150 years, coins in poor condition (unless they are of very rare dates) will not only not be sought after, but are almost certain to exceed the demand for them and, again, will only command low prices, in some cases little more than their face value.

To illustrate the effect of condition on value let us examine the prices quoted in up-to-date catalogues for some of the copper, bronze, brass and silver coins issued during this century.

Brass Threepences of Elizabeth II

It is most important to note that as these coins are, numismatically speaking, very modern and as none is extremely rare, or even very rare, a standard catalogue does not quote prices for them in grades lower than Very Fine. (I have ignored coins dated 1967, as these are so numerous and so easily obtained, even in Brilliant Uncirculated condition, that they are not worth more than face value at the time of writing.)

Year	Mintage	EF	UNC
1953	30,618,000		
1954	41,720,000	£1·50	£2·50
1955	41,075,200	1·50	2·50
1956	36,801,600	1·50	2·50
1957	24,294,400	1·00	1·50
1958	20,504,000	2·00	5·00
1959	28,499,200	1·00	1·50
1960	83,078,400	0·75	1·25
1961	41,102,400		0·30
1962	51,545,600		0·30
1963	39,482,866		0·20
1964	44,867,200		0·20
1965	27,160,000		0·25
1966	53,160,000		0·10

At least five significant points emerge from study of the above figures:

1. The prices for the coins dated 1958 are higher than for the other years. This is obviously due to the relatively low mintage for that year.

2. The 1965 coin, though still only catalogued at 25p is valued at more than twice as much as those of 1963, 1964 and 1966. This could obviously be due to its relatively low mintage compared with the other three years quoted – which makes it similar to the 1958 issue and also makes it a coin of greater potential growth in value in the future.

3. Coins dated as far back as 1961 are not, *as yet*, considered worth collecting in less than Uncirculated condition.

4. An improvement by one grade on average nearly doubles its value.

5. Notwithstanding what has been said about low mintages causing values to rise, it will be seen that in 1960, though the official issue was 83,078,400, the coin is now catalogued at approximately four times the value of that of 1961, when only approximately half the number of coins were issued. This apparent contradiction may be due to the circumstance described on pages 15–16.

Let us go one reign further back and look at the brass threepenny bits of George VI. The coins are catalogued as on page 21.

Year	Mintage	F	VF	EF
1937	45,707,957		·15	£0·75
1938	14,532,332		·75	2·50
1939	5,603,021		1·00	3·50
1940	12,636,018		·50	2·00
1941	60,239,489		·25	1·50
1942	103,214,400		·25	1·50
1943	101,702,400		·25	1·50
1944	69,760,000		·25	1·50
1945	33,942,466		·25	1·50
1946	620,734	£1·00	6·00	35·00
1948	4,230,400	0·25	1·25	5·00
1949	464,000	1·50	10·00	50·00
1950	1,600,000	0·30	2·50	9·00
1951	1,184,000	0·40	3·25	20·00
1952	25,494,400		0·30	1·00

These figures emphasize another most significant factor – *modern coins even of rare dates, are not considered particularly valuable if in less than very fine condition.*

This point is shown most clearly in the coins dated 1946 and 1949. In 1946 the value in Fine condition is £1·00 but the same coin one grade better is six times as valuable, and with the 1949 issue the Very Fine coin is valued at more than six times the Fine value.

This grade-price differential is perhaps most noticeable in small-denomination copper and bronze coins but the principle still applies with all coins, as is shown by the following further extract from *Seaby's Standard Catalogue of British Coins* (1972).

Year	Coin	F	VF	EF
1902	sixpence	£0·75	£2·00	£5·00
1905	shilling	9·00	25·00	55·00
1905	florin	7·50	20·00	50·00
1905	halfcrown	20·00	75·00	240·00
1844	crown	5·00	17·50	85·00
1817	half-sovereign	10·00	20·00	35·00
1819	sovereign	750·00	1,250·00	2,000·00

These figures suggest some further points:

1. The face value or denomination of a coin is of less importance in determining its value than a combination of rarity and condition. For instance, a 1905 halfcrown is valued at considerably more than an 1844 crown.

2. The age of a coin does not automatically make it more valuable: the 1905 shilling, for instance, is worth much more than many Roman or Greek coins 2,000 or more years older.

3. The scarcer a coin is, the greater is the difference in actual money between one grade and another. The 1819 sovereign is very rare and the difference between its value in EF condition and that in VF condition is £750. However, the *proportional* difference may not be as great – compare the grade differences, percentage-wise, of the sixpence and the sovereign.

All of this means that coins in the highest grades are likely to increase most in value, and the collector should therefore always endeavour to buy the best condition coin he can afford – and perhaps equally, if not more importantly, *do his utmost to prevent them deteriorating* by unwise handling or inadequate methods of storage.

CHAPTER FOUR

Market Rises and Recessions

About five or six years ago, due mainly, it is thought, to the approaching adoption of decimal currency in Great Britain, there was a tremendous increase in coin-collecting. People felt, with some justification, that when the new decimal money came into use the values of pre-decimal currency would rise as more and more of it was withdrawn from circulation.

Consequently coin prices rose, sometimes at a fantastic rate. This was accelerated by coin speculators who bought in great quantities and thus accentuated the shortage.

At about the same time there was talk of devaluation in the air and this led to an urgent demand from speculators for pre-1920 silver coins (which had a 92·5% silver content); advertisers were offering as much as 50s. (£2·50) per £1 face value for these coins *in any condition*. Quite apart from the profit they would make by reselling the coins for bullion, there was always the chance that some of the coins they received might be of numismatic value.

Ordinary collectors soon found the prices of coins in Extremely Fine or Uncirculated condition beyond their reach, and they often had to be content with lower grades. The additional demand for lower-grade coins caused their prices to rise in turn, though not quite so much as those in the top grades, for there were of course more poor coins than good ones.

As recounted in Chapter Two, the Government tried to curb the speculators' activities in 1967 by decreeing that all non-decimal coins issued between that year and full decimalization in February 1971 would be dated 1967. The chances of 1967 coins rising in value diminished at once almost to nil and the speculators began to release their stocks as quickly as possible in the hope of making at least some profit before the prices fell or to cut their losses.

Inevitably coin values decreased and particularly in the lower grades, for with increased supplies of better-grade coins nobody wanted to buy those in inferior condition.

As a result a large number of genuine collectors saw the market value of many of their coins decrease, sometimes alarmingly so. As always, however, prices slowly began to stabilize and at the present time there are signs that prices are beginning to rise again, though this trend is still only really evident in the top-grades.

Now is the time to begin to buy good-condition coins again, following the general rule about buying when prices are low and selling when they are high.

The difficulty, of course, is to know the right moment to buy or sell. There is no infallible method of doing this but there are certain methods you can use which will eliminate at least some of the element of chance.

You can subscribe to one or more of the following journals which give the current values of a wide variety of coins and from which you can make your own analyses of market trends, and also obtain a regular check on the market selling prices of your own coins.

Modern Coins and Banknotes (Spink), published 5 times a year, by subscription;

Seaby's Coin and Medal Bulletin, published monthly, by subscription;

The Numismatic Circular (Spink), published monthly;

Coin Monthly (Numismatic Publishing Co.), published monthly;

Coins (Link House Publications), published monthly;

Coin Collectors Weekly.

An excellent way of watching the progress of a particular coin or group of coins is by means of a graph. If you trace the passage of time on the horizontal axis and price on the vertical one, you can tell by the steepness of the graph how fast the price is rising or falling. This method does not, of course, predict: it indicates a general tendency, and it remains up to you, the collector, to interpret the evidence.

Another method of spotting potential rises in values is to study the advertisements or notices of publishers indicating the forthcoming publication of new books and catalogues (not reprints of annual catalogues).

An excellent example of this occurred recently when within a very short period three new catalogues on the coinage of Ireland appeared almost concurrently with a rise in values of the coins of that country. The Eire coinage, long neglected by collectors, came into favour when the prices of high-grade British coins rose sharply and became beyond the reach of the average person. This trend was either anticipated by the professional numismatists or detected immediately it began to show, and almost immediately they concentrated on producing catalogues which they expected would soon be in demand.

B

THE MECHANICS OF COLLECTING

CHAPTER FIVE

Buying

Antique Shops and Market Stalls

A few years ago it was often possible to pick up coins from antique shops and market stalls at very reasonable and sometimes bargain prices, but with the enormous expansion of interest in coin collecting over the last few years such opportunities have become the exception rather than the rule. Indeed in many markets there are regular stalls run by coin dealers who know to within very close limits the market value of the coins they have on show; and you can be almost certain that even the owners of junk stalls who have a few coins on a tray amidst the other items also know their current values, and will have copies of current price lists or coin catalogues tucked away.

Nevertheless it always pays to have a look around; you may find just the coin you are looking for in the condition you want, and stall owners, as distinct from old-fashioned dealers in permanent premises, are often open to offers and prepared to bring down the marked price of a coin in order to make a quick sale and reduce their tied-up capital.

Buying from Private Individuals

Before you can buy a coin from a private individual (other than a personal friend) it is essential, first, that he should know that you are a potential purchaser and second, and in my opinion of equal importance, he must know you to be a person of integrity who will give him a fair price for his coin. Quite apart from any ethical considerations, this will encourage him to sell to you, not only on this but on any subsequent occasions.

There is a variety of ways in which you can publicise your interest in buying coins. You can, for example, put a small advertisement in a local newspaper or in a newsagent's window. The wording can be quite simple; e.g. 'Private Collector Pays Fair Price For Excellent Condition Victorian Coins. Telephone: XYZ 3456'. Do not give your private address.

There are several reasons for this latter point. Everybody who reads your notice will know that you are a collector and possibly keep coins in your house, which could be of interest to thieves. Furthermore before many days have passed you will have people knocking at your door with tins of out-of-change coins late at night, in the middle of your favourite television programme or during your Sunday lunch.

A preliminary telephone conversation with a potential seller will help you decide whether you are interested in what he has to sell. It will also give you an opportunity to warn him not to clean his coins. Some years ago I put in a Cornish newspaper an advertisement like the one above, and among the many calls I received was one from an old lady near Redruth who claimed to have a number of excellent-condition Victorian 'Bun' pennies and Old Head bronze coins. I arranged to see her the following day. She had been quite right about her coins; they were in at least Extremely Fine condition, but every one was brightly polished. 'I couldn't sell you dirty coins,' she explained, 'so my daughter and I spent all yesterday evening polishing them up with Duraglit.'

A slower, but very effective kind of publicity is through the personal recommendation of your friends or people from whom you have already bought coins. The value of this method is the establishment of yourself as a person of integrity, which is of immeasurable worth.

A sometimes effective, but not generally recommended, method is by literally going from door to door in a selected area and asking whether the inhabitants of the house have any good-condition coins they wish to sell.

A Fair Price

My suggested advertisement, above, states that a fair price will be given, but what is a fair price?

A professional dealer will ordinarily pay from one-half to two thirds of catalogue value (which, as every reputable catalogue explains, are the dealer's *selling* prices) according to how badly he wants the coin.

It is my opinion that if you have advertised for coins of a certain grading or standard and you are offered them by a member of the public, then you should pay not less and almost certainly more – even if only a little more – than two-thirds of their catalogue values.

Once you have established a reputation for paying fair prices, the news soon gets around, and you will find that people with coins to sell will come to you without your having to advertise.

In such circumstances, the only disputes which are liable to arise are over questions of grading of the coins which are offered to you. People with little or no numismatic knowledge or experience invariably over-grade their coins and are apt to describe as Mint or Nearly Mint any coin on which there are no blatantly obvious signs of wear. It is useful, therefore, to carry about with you, or have immediately available, a set of clearly labelled and meticulously graded coins which you can compare with the state of those offered.

Buying from Dealers

There is much to be said for buying coins from *reputable* coin dealers. I stress the word 'reputable' for, in recent years, a number of somewhat dubious dealers have set themselves up in business in an attempt to cash in on the boom in coin collecting. I must, however, make it absolutely clear that *most* new coin dealers *are* reputable; after all the highly reputable firms of today such as Baldwin, Seaby and Spink, were once new firms themselves.

With such old-established firms one can buy safely from them, even by post, for their gradings are almost invariably exact and their coins are authentic; if, by any very remote chance, a coin is proved to be other than it is advertised to be, it will be withdrawn or changed without question.

In general, however, it is always most strongly advisable to buy a coin in person, for then you can inspect it at leisure and perhaps compare it with other coins of the same denomination.

Admittedly, you will almost certainly have to pay more than you would have done buying privately, but the rate of appreciation of a personally selected coin you have chosen with care from a good selection should soon wipe out the extra amount which you have paid.

Another advantage of buying from a dealer is that over a period of time you can develop a firm business relationship. Furthermore he will get to know the types of coins in which you are interested, will look out for them and let you know when one comes onto the market or in his stock. Thus you will be able to acquire good specimen coins which you might otherwise have missed.

Be extremely careful about postal buying from firms not known to you. Usually firms dealing in postal selling allow you so many days to inspect the coin before either sending off your money for the purchase price or returning the coin. If you do not return the coin by the date specified it will be assumed that you are satisfied with it and any money you have paid will not be returned (and most dealers to whom you are not known personally will, quite rightly, expect you to send the money with your order).

However, you must be extremely careful to study the actual number of days in which you can have the coin in your possession. If, for instance, a period of seven days is mentioned, you must check whether this period of time is counted from the dealer's date of posting to the date when he receives it back from you or whether the number of days mentioned is exclusive of the time the coin is in the post. This is particularly important in view of the present, often most unsatisfactory, postal service.

A final word of warning about dealing by post: though all coins which are sent to you should come by registered post, there is no guarantee that the envelope either contains the coin you have requested or that it contains a coin at all. It is wise, therefore, when you receive a registered letter or parcel, to open it in the presence of the postman to check that it contains the item which you have asked the firm to send.

I speak from experience on this matter, for some time ago a person sent, or said he sent (quite unsolicited), a coin for my inspection. I opened the letter in front of two witnesses, but though the packing was inside, there was no coin. The sender then proceeded to demand it back. Though the coin which was supposed to have been sent was worth only a few pounds, the situation began to get a little difficult – including a visit by a policeman (very friendly) – until further inquiries revealed that the complaining individual had apparently been making quite a habit of the practice in various parts of the country.

Buying at Coin Auctions

There are two main types of coin auctions; postal, where one studies a catalogue beforehand and then sends in a bid for a particular coin; and the normal kind, which one can attend in person and inspect the items sent in for sale. Postal bids can, of course, also be made for coins to be sold at a normal auction or, alternatively, you can arrange for a dealer or some other person to attend the auction and bid on your behalf.

In general it is better to confine one's buying activities to those auctions which are run by experienced specialist firms and which you can attend in person after having inspected the coins in which you are interested.

The disadvantages of buying at an auction are twofold: first, you do not often get a real bargain, for prices tend to approximate to catalogue values, and secondly, unless you are very careful, emotion can overcome discretion in the excitement of trying to acquire the coin you desire.

The only sensible procedure is to obtain a catalogue of the sale as far in advance as possible; study it carefully (particularly the conditions of sale, which should always be included), and mark off the coins for which you intend to bid. It is especially important to note whether the auctioneers guarantee that if a coin should subsequently be found to be different from the catalogue description, the purchase price will be refunded automatically, for a number of excellent forgeries of ancient and gold coins are at present being introduced into the market. Some of these forgeries are so good that they have deceived even expert numismatists and only been exposed by careful, detailed and even microscopic inspection.

Next, study up-to-date catalogues which give the values of coins in a variety of grades, along with any other auction reports and dealers' circulars or bulletins which give coin prices. Having done this, try to estimate what you consider to be a reasonable price for the coins you are contemplating buying and mark this price on your catalogue along with, if you so desire, the maximum price which you are prepared to pay. This may be less or more than the first price you have marked, but having decided on this price, and having examined the coin(s) to confirm your estimate and judgement, do not exceed this when you make your bids at the actual sale.

Remember always that, with certain few exceptions, there will probably be similar coins at future auctions, and that failing to obtain a coin at one auction does not mean that your opportunity of obtaining such a coin has gone for ever.

In short, let your head and not your heart rule your bidding.

CHAPTER SIX

Selling

As I am assuming that you are, first and foremost, a collector who wishes to ensure that whatever you buy for your own collection is likely to increase and not decrease in value over the years, then I must equally assume that you will normally only sell your coins if either they are surplus to your requirements or you need money to buy another coin.

Let me give an example. I specialize in the Victorian period and am endeavouring to complete a type-set of Victoria, with every coin in at least Extremely Fine or Uncirculated condition.

Some Victorian coins in these conditions are extremely expensive. For instance, a Young Head crown in EF condition would cost nearly £100, and considerably more if it is Uncirculated. However, rather than have a gap in my collection, I might buy a Young Head crown which is only in Fine condition, my aim being to replace it as soon as possible with one of a better grade.

Whenever I had the opportunity of buying other coins, Victorian or otherwise, which I considered to be reasonable bargains, or new sets of coins which I felt certain would show a fairly rapid increase in value, I would buy them with one main aim in view: to sell them at a profit so that I could buy an EF Young Head crown.

Such a practice, I consider, does not make me a dealer, whose whole business is the buying and selling of coins purely for profit, but (I hope) a sensible collector who will ultimately build up a desirable collection of Victorian coins at very little cost.

Broadly speaking there are three ways of disposing of a coin: by selling to a dealer; by selling to another private collector; or by putting it in an auction.

Selling to Dealers

A lot of collectors grumble at the prices that dealers offer them for their coins. Only too often, however, it turns out they have overgraded their coins absurdly. Also, they seem to expect to receive catalogue prices – which is to say the dealer's selling prices – although they would not be surprised to be offered much less for their second-hand car than they paid for it. They know that the car's value is bound to drop, but that a coin's value is likely to increase. However, they make no allowance for the considerations that affect a dealer's buying price – his overheads, his profit, his stock of the coin in question and how easily he can resell it. Moreover the values of coins do not always increase, and a dealer who is unable to resell a coin for some time may find that his profit has been eaten up by a recession.

However, if you offer your coins for sale to a reputable dealer you can expect to receive a fair price, and you should not offer them unless you expect to take that price. This is important to bear in mind because, if you turn down the offer, the dealer may well charge you a fee for valuing your coins – and in my view he is quite justified.

The principal advantage of selling to a dealer is that you are paid immediately – by contrast with selling through an auction; you have no advertising costs to bear and you have none of the bother of hunting round for a private buyer who will make you a sensible offer on the spot.

As with buying coins, always sell, if possible, to dealers who have been long established or about whom you have had good and reliable reports.

As a general rule do not send coins to dealers who advertise and use box numbers only, or where the address given in the advertisement is that of some hotel. Such people could disappear overnight, taking your coins with them. There are, of course, exceptions to this rule. For instance, some of the internationally known and long established dealers advertise that Mr X, their representative, is intending making a buying tour of say, Lancashire or Devon, and that for a certain length of time he will be staying at such and such an hotel where you may send or take coins; your coins will be as safe in his hands as if you had taken or sent them to the dealer's permanent head-quarters. It is, of course, always advisable to take the coins to the dealer yourself.

In the past it has not been, and still is not, unknown for a collector to send a coin to an advertiser, only to receive it back a few days later with a note saying that the coin was not suitable because it was of too low a grade. This seems quite fair and reasonable, but for one important thing: the coin which you receive back is not the coin you sent. You may *know* this, but it is well nigh impossible to prove. Though such cases are few and far between, when they do happen the sins of one disreputable dealer are apt to be attributed to them all. So I must repeat, most dealers are eminently respectable people and follow a very strict code of ethics.

Selling to Private Collectors

The advantage of selling a coin privately is that you may receive a better price than you might receive elsewhere. The buyer knows, or should know, how much he would have to pay at a dealer's or an auctioneer's and, if you are offering a coin in good condition, he may be happy to pay something above the dealer's buying price, although it is unlikely that he will pay more than the dealer's selling price.

You can attract buyers by a variety of means. Advertisement in a numismatic journal or local newspaper is often very effective. It should be carefully worded, though, so as not to attract burglars, nor tell them where you live.

Another way of selling coins is through a coin club. I believe collectors should always join such clubs, for there one can meet fellow collectors with whom one can discuss matters of common numismatic interest, and buy and sell coins. It is also a common practice at club meetings to hold small auction sales.

Selling at Coin Auctions

Generally, though not always, the best prices for your coins can be obtained by selling them at a coin auction run by specialist coin auctioneers. The prices realized approximate to, and sometimes exceed, those published in conservative coin catalogues such as those published by B. A. Seaby Ltd.

Certain of the larger auctioneers – Glendining & Co. Ltd, for example – are normally only prepared to accept coins whose total value, *in their estimation*, is likely to exceed, say, £30. Their estimation is of some importance, for, quite rightly, they grade coins very severely indeed. By doing this they maintain their reputation for grading, and the numismatic world knows that if one of their catalogues says a coin is Very Fine, there will be no doubt whatsoever about it, and that it will certainly be nearer Extremely Fine than a good Fine. This can be a little disappointing to the would-be seller, but it is better to undergrade a coin and be pleasantly surprised than to overgrade it.

Auctioneers deduct a commission, normally between ten and fifteen per cent of the price realized at the auction.

Assuming that your coin realizes approximately catalogue value, you will receive about 85% of the dealer's selling price, compared with the average maximum of $66\frac{2}{3}$% which you would receive from the dealer himself. Remember, however, that if you sell to a dealer you will get your money immediately, whereas if you sell your coin by auction you might well have to wait a month, or even two, before your coin comes up for sale, and another week or fourteen days before you receive settlement.

However, and this is not generally realized, most large and reputable coin auctioneers are prepared to pay you a sum on account *immediately*, providing the potential auction value of the coin is fairly large.

Not all auctioneers set a minimal potential sale value on the coins they are prepared to accept for sale; and some country auctioneers, and some in London too, are prepared to accept single coins or very small collections.

There are, of course, possible disappointments for both seller and auctioneer in these circumstances, for the price realized for a relatively poor coin could be so low that after deduction of commission the seller receives less than the face value of the coin.

Be careful not to set too high a reserve price on any coins you submit for auction, for there is always a danger that they may not be sold and, in such a case, you may be liable to pay a commission fee – usually 5% of your reserve price.

It is, however, a fairly common practice for coins not sold at one sale to be automatically included in the next, when you will be asked if you wish to maintain or change your reserve price.

Some people are firmly of the opinion that if they state a reserve price the coin is not likely to make more than that price, but this is far from true. However, if it does not make that price, or only just makes it, the seller has no real solid foundation for complaint, for he is the one that set it; and one must assume that, though he would like to receive a sum in excess of the reserve price, he must have been of the opinion, when deciding on the figure, that it was worth selling at that price.

It must also be remembered that if you put a coin up for auction there is no reason why you should not attend the actual auction and bid for it yourself so as to increase the price realized; the danger, however, is knowing just when to stop, for if you are not careful, you could end up buying your own coin and paying the auctioneer's commission into the bargain.

In the chapter on buying coins I suggested that, in general, it was better always to buy at places where you could inspect the coins. I would also suggest that it is better to sell your coins at public rather than at postal auctions where, not only can they not be seen by potential buyers, but you yourself have no certain check on the bids sent in by post.

CHAPTER SEVEN

Essential Equipment

Most newcomers to any particular hobby or interest tend to get so carried away by their enthusiasm that they will buy almost anything that seems even half useful. There *are* certain items of equipment which are absolutely necessary, but they are not many and need not cost a lot of money. Basically they are:

a magnifying glass;
catalogues;
reference books;
and storage equipment.

Magnifying Glass

This is absolutely essential for close inspection of your coins, both for interest and for the purpose of assessing their condition. It need not cost a lot of money. For a first general inspection of a coin I use a three-inch lens which I picked up on a stall in a local market for 5s.; such lenses can often be bought in shops which sell surplus WD stores, electric motors, wireless parts and so on.

For closer inspection a Gowland magnifying glass, obtainable from any dealer, is the invaluable every day instrument of the professional numismatist.

The Gowland glass folds inside a metal cover for protection when not in use; a large lens like that mentioned above should have some means of protection, such as a soft leather or cloth bag.

Catalogues and Reference Books

Among the following list of recommended catalogues you should find one or more that suits your needs.

GREAT BRITAIN

Standard Catalogue of British Coins, ed. P. J. Seaby
British Copper Coins and Their Values, P. J. Seaby and M. Bussell
A Guide Book of English Coins, 19th and 20th Centuries, K. E. Bressett
The Crown Pieces of Great Britain, H. W. A. Linecar
English Proof and Pattern Crown-size Pieces, H. W. A. Linecar and A. G. Stone

IRELAND

The Guide Book to the Coinage of Ireland, A. Dowle and P. Finn
Coins and Tokens of Ireland, P. J. Seaby

CLASSICAL COINS

Roman Coins and their Values, D. R. Sear
An Outline of Ancient Greek Coins, Z. H. Klawans

GENERAL

Coins of the World, 1750–1850, W. D. Craig
A Catalogue of Modern World Coins, R. S. Yeoman
Current Coins of the World, R. S. Yeoman
British Commonwealth Coins, 1649–1971, J. Remick, S. James, P. Finn and A. Dowle
Gold Coins of the World from 600 AD, R. Friedberg
Gold Coins of Europe since 1700, H. Schlumberger

Reference Books

The following selection of books may not be vital in the early days of collecting but they are invaluable as sources of more detailed information than will usually be found in the normal catalogues.

English Silver Coinage from 1649, H. A. Seaby and P. A. Rayner
English Copper, Tin and Bronze Coins in the British Museum, C. W. Peck
Beginner's Guide to Coin Collecting, H. W. A. Linecar
An Advanced Guide to Coin Collecting, H. W. A. Linecar
Collecting Modern British Coins, J. Edmundson
Coins: Ancient, Mediaeval and Modern, R. A. G. Carson
The Crown Pieces of Great Britain and the Commonwealth, H. W. A. Linecar
A Start to Coin Collecting, Margaret Amstell

There are, of course, many more excellent and specialized books on many aspects of numismatics. Leaflets, catalogues and brochures giving lists of such books can be obtained on request from B. A. Seaby Ltd, Audley House, 11 Margaret Street, London W1 and from Spink and Son Ltd, 5 King Street, St James's, London SW1.

Coin Storage Equipment

As the value of a coin is largely dependent upon its condition it is absolutely essential to prevent it from deteriorating, and it must be protected both against atmospheric pollution and from contact with other coins. The most common methods of protection are described below.

Paper and Plastic Envelopes

Small square envelopes made of a special type of paper (approximate cost 15p per 100) or in transparent plastic (about 62½p per 100) are commonly used for holding coins. The advantage of paper envelopes is that details of the coin inside can be written on the outside; the disadvantage is that the coin always has to be taken out – i.e. handled – for inspection. A coin kept in a plastic envelope can be inspected without handling, but it is difficult to write details on the plastic envelope except with a chinagraph pencil, which tends to smear. Both the paper and the plastic envelopes can be stored in the sort of metal or plastic boxes that are used for holding 2″ × 2″ photographic transparencies; these can be bought relatively cheaply.

A useful development, which combines the advantages of both the plastic and paper envelopes, is a system whereby the plastic envelope has an additional pocket into which is slipped a small card on which details of the coin can be written, the envelopes being stored in a special box.

Albums and Cases

For further protection, and easy transportation, it is advisable to keep one's coins in an album or case.

The former is the more portable, and a comparatively recent innovation. It is a book whose leaves are divided into a number of pockets, usually of transparent plastic, so that the coins are both protected and displayed. Albums come in all sizes, from that which will fit into a pocket to extremely large, opulent and costly versions. Many are designed to contain a particular kind of collection, such as a type-set.

A wide variety of albums is available, but the collector must ensure that whichever one he buys provides complete protection, allows the obverse and reverse of the coin to be seen without handling and holds the coins securely, at the same time permitting them to be easily removed.

The coin case or cabinet is a small chest of shallow drawers, each containing several coins. Each drawer is lined with a thin board pierced with round holes in which the coins lie, or is divided into 'boxes' by thin strips of wood, so that the coins are prevented from sliding about. The holes, or the squares that the strips form, vary in size to accommodate different types of coin, and are lined with felt or velvet. The details of each coin may be noted on a cardboard disc, that is put with the coin in its place; you can make your own discs, but they are commercially available at modest cost.

Coin cases vary very much in price; inexpensive plastic versions are available, while at the other end of the scale are fine pieces of cabinet-making which command high prices like any other sort of furniture.

CHAPTER EIGHT

Records and Insurance

It is absolutely essential that you should keep an accurate and fairly detailed record of all your coins, both for the purpose of insurance and to keep track of your buying and selling transactions.

There are a number of first-class commercially produced record books and coin recording systems, many of them advertised in the numismatic journals. Of course you may prefer to devise your own record system, which can be kept quite satisfactorily in a notebook while your collection is still small.

The nine essential facts which need to be recorded are as below and as set out overleaf:

1. Description of the coin, including a catalogue reference number.
2. The grade of the coin.
3. Where and/or from whom the coin was obtained.
4. The date of purchase.
5. The buying price.
6. The present catalogue value (year by year) of the coin.
7. To whom sold.
8. Price received.   } If you ever do sell your coins.
9. Profit (or loss) on the sale.

Insuring Your Coins

It is of course sheer common sense to insure your coins. From a burglar's point of view they are ideal – portable, comparatively easily sold, often very valuable for their size and weight. They are also easily damaged by fire, accidents and so on. The essential thing is to know at a stated date each year (preferably

Your record might look like this:

VICTORIAN PENNIES

No.	Date, Description and Notes	Grade	Where and When Obtained	Buying Price	Selling Price	Gain or Loss	Present Value		
							1972	1973	1974
1	1841 Seaby's Cat. No. 3186	EF	from J. Brown Esq. Watford, 1968	£8·00					
2	1844 Seaby's Cat. No. 3186	VF	As above	£2·00	£3·00	+£1·00			
3	1860 Seaby's Cat. No. 3192 First Bronze Issue	EF	Auction. Black & Co. London 1969	£12·00					
4	1881 Seaby's Cat. No. 3192 a. 'H' be ow date	EF	Gift from H. Green Esq.	Nil					
5	1898 Seaby's Cat. No. 3196 Some lustre, slight edge knock	EF	From H. White, Truro	£7·00	£9·00	+£2·00			

(Note that in the description column I have put a Seaby's *Standard Catalogue of British Coins* reference number. This not only defines the exact coin entered but also saves a considerable time in making entries.)

just before your insurance premium is due) the present value of your collection and its estimated value one year ahead. It is wise to insure the coins for the amount of the future value.

If you have kept detailed records like that suggested above for four or five years, you will have little difficulty in assessing approximate future values.

In many cases insurance companies require a separate list of any coins which are catalogued at more than £5.

The cost of insurance of coins is largely dependent upon where they are kept. If, for instance, they are kept at your bank and only withdrawn for short periods, the cost will be less than if you keep them in your own home; furthermore, if your collection is a valuable one and you wish to keep it at home, the company may insist that it be kept in a safe of approved pattern. The premium may also be higher if you wish to carry your coins from place to place during the year.

However, whatever the cost may be, insurance is imperative. The company that insures your house will normally cover your coins as well, but if you have difficulties about this, a reputable coin dealer will be able to advise you.

CHAPTER NINE

Where to Seek Advice

The main sources of advice and information available to the ordinary coin collector are:

Members of the many coin clubs and numismatic societies to be found in most countries of the world.

Professional coin dealers.

The curators of museums in which there are reasonably sized collections of coins and (in Great Britain) The Department of Coins and Medals, The British Museum, London W C 1.

The official Government department or organization concerned with the minting of coinage – in Great Britain it is The Royal Mint, Tower Hill, London E C 3.

Standard catalogues and reference books, along with numismatic journals published weekly, monthly or annually.

Coin Clubs

In nearly every town and city of this and many other countries there are coin clubs or numismatic societies. Their members are those of the public interested (but not expertly informed) in collecting coins, long-standing numismatists with expert knowledge and professional coin dealers (who often offer discounts on purchases to members of their own club).

Details of such clubs can usually be obtained from local coin dealers and museums, through accounts of their activities in local newspapers and national magazines and journals, or by writing to the Secretary of any national organisation of coin clubs in your own country. In Great Britain, particulars of clubs can be obtained from the *Coin Year Book* 1972 (Numismatic Publishing Company, Brentwood, Essex. 75p) published annually.

The most learned society in Great Britain is The Royal Numismatic Society, membership of which can only be obtained by being proposed and seconded by Fellows of the Society and balloted for at one of their regular meetings. Details can be obtained from The Secretary, The Royal Numismatic Society, c/o The Department of Coins and Medals, The British Museum, London W C1.

For those interested in the collecting of banknotes, membership of the International Bank Note Society is almost indispensible. Particulars can be obtained from Mr F. Philipson, 5 Windermere Road, Beeston, Nottingham, NG9 3AS.

Professional Coin Dealers

Dealers are always willing to give both the new and the experienced collector advice on building up a coin collection which will have economic-growth potential.

Remember, however, that if, as a casual and as yet unknown person to them, you seek advice on the values of your coins, they are likely to charge you a fee, and rightly so, for a valuation, particularly of a rare coin, takes time and expertise.

Museums

In any museum with a reasonably large collection of coins you will almost certainly find someone expert in numismatics, from whom general advice or coin-identification can be sought, or, failing that, a member of the staff who will put you in contact with someone who can help you.

You can send (by registered post) or take your coins to The British Museum's Department of Coins and Medals for identification and authentication, or seek general advice from them. The Department's experts (who are always very helpful indeed) are not permitted to value coins; that is the concern of the coin dealer or some knowledgeable private numismatist.

The Museum makes no charge for its services, but no museum's resources are limitless, and I would recommend that you reserve your thornier problems for them, and seek day-to-day advice elsewhere.

The Royal Mint

In Great Britain, British coins or coins struck at the Mint can be sent for authentication. If you have, say, what you think is a genuine 1933 penny or an example of the almost-mythical 1937 Edward VIII brass threepenny piece and you send it to the Royal Mint, they will tell you whether or not it is a genuine Royal Mint-produced coin. As with the British Museum, they will not value your coin, nor do they charge for their services of this nature.

Many other countries offer the same facilities at their own Mints.

Standard Catalogues, Reference Books and Journals

If you cannot afford to buy (and it is difficult for many people to do so these days) *all* the books you require for the particular category of coin you are interested in they can usually be studied at your local reference library. In many cases general books on numismatics can be borrowed through a lending library.

There are, of course, certain books which are almost indispensible and which you should have by you at all times. My suggested short list is on pp. 41–42, and most of the items on it are not expensive.

In many libraries you may also find and study various of the weekly and monthly numismatic journals. It should always be borne in mind, however, that it is advisable to subscribe to at least one of the monthly journals, for there is a double benefit; you can study it at leisure in your own home and you are building up a valuable private reference library by relatively cheap monthly instalments.

THE COINS TO COLLECT

CHAPTER TEN

Proofs

I have stressed the point that the serious collector and numismatist always tries to obtain coins in the best possible condition and, whenever such are obtainable, in either FDC (Fleur de Coin) or Brilliant Uncirculated condition, for not only are such coins objects of beauty, they are also excellent investment prospects because there is always a demand for them.

Proof coins and sets almost invariably come in the FDC grading *at the time of issue*. Furthermore the issues are also limited in number, and therefore fulfil the second condition for value-growth: the demand is greater than the supply. Their values, therefore, will automatically increase.

One point must be made clear. 'Proof' is not a coin grade such as Uncirculated or Extremely Fine, but indicates a special *type* of coin. Proofs are coins struck, almost individually, from specially prepared, highly polished dies and usually have a plain edge (in the case of crowns there is often a raised or an incused, or cut-in, inscription around the edge) and a mirror-like field. Often the design has a 'frosted' appearance produced by treating the incuse parts of the die with a weak solution of acid; in some cases the whole coin is given a matt surface.

Proofs are usually issued at the beginning of a new reign or when the coinage design is changed during a reign, and are normally housed by the issuing Mint in special cases or boxes.

Proofs must be distinguished from Specimen sets, such as those issued by the Royal Mint on the first introduction of the new British decimal coinage. These specimen sets are made up from Brilliant Uncirculated normal-issue coins, and can, and often do, contain coins with slight blemishes and surface scratches caused by contact with other coins during the minting and packaging operations.

Though today proofs are issued by the Royal Mint, prior to 1887 they were issued by the actual engravers.

In addition to official and publicly issued proof sets and individual coins (such as crowns) it is believed that it is the practice of the Royal Mint every year to strike a very small number of proofs of each denomination issued during that particular year. Such coins are extremely scarce and rarely come on the market; when they do, they can command very high prices.

As a proof is a type of coin and not a grading, one can obtain Proof coins in conditions varying from FDC down to Fair or even Poor, depending on how they have been handled (or mishandled) over the years. Low-grade proof coins will normally be of little interest either to collectors or dealers, and therefore of very little value compared with specimens in the higher grades.

The table below lists the proof sets issued in this country over approximately the last 150 years, and their present catalogue values.

Reign, Date of Issue	Issues	Present Catalogue Value of set (FDC)
George IV 1826	New issue. Five pounds to Farthing (11 coins). About 400 sets issued.	£1,850
William IV 1831	Coronation issue. Two pounds to farthing (14 coins). Exact number of sets issued not known, but over 120.	£1,850
Victoria 1839	Young Head. 'Una and the Lion'. Five pounds and sovereign to farthing (15 coins). About 300 sets issued.	£1,850
Victoria 1853	Sovereign to farthing, including 'Gothic' Crown (16 coins). Issue not known, but very few.	£2,000

Reign, Date of Issue	Issues	Present Catalogue Value of set (FDC)
Victoria 1887	(*a*) Golden Jubilee issue. Five pounds to threepence (11 coins). 797 sets issued.	£750
	(*b*) Golden Jubilee issue (short silver set). Crown to threepence (7 coins). 287 sets issued.	£225
Victoria 1893	(*a*) Old Head issue. Five-pounds to three-pence (10 coins). 756 sets issued.	£800
	(*b*) Old Head (short silver set). Halfcrown to threepence (6 coins). 556 sets issued.	£200
Edward VII 1902	(*a*) Coronation set (long set). Five pounds to Maundy penny, matt surface (13 coins). 8,066 sets issued.	£350
	(*b*) Coronation (short set). Sovereign to Maundy penny, matt surface (11 coins). 7,057 sets issued.	£125
George V 1911	(*a*) Coronation (long set). Five pounds to Maundy penny (12 coins). 2,812 sets issued.	£450
	(*b*) Coronation (short set). Sovereign to Maundy penny (10 coins). 952 sets issued.	£175
	(*c*) Coronation set. Halfcrown to Maundy penny (8 coins). 2,243 sets issued.	£100
George V 1927	New-type coinage. Crown to threepence (6 coins). 15,000 sets issued.	£85
George VI 1937	(*a*) Coronation gold set. Five pounds to half-sovereign (4 coins). 5,501 sets issued.	£325
	(*b*) Coronation silver and bronze set. Crown to farthing, including Maundy money (15 coins). 20,901 sets issued.	£42·50
George VI 1950	Mid-century set. Halfcrown to farthing (9 coins). 17,513 sets issued.	£25
George VI 1951	Festival of Britain set. Crown to farthing (10 coins). 20,000 sets issued.	£37·50
Elizabeth II 1953	Coronation set. Crown to farthing (10 coins). 40,000 sets issued.	£25

I mentioned above that it has been the practice of the Royal Mint to strike a number of proof sets each year and that these can command high prices. The same applies to proofs of individual coins, as is shown by the following examples:

At the time of writing the *selling* value of a 1949 proof set (halfcrown to farthing) is £600; and that of a 1960 proof crown is £85, and of a special 'satin' finish 1965 Churchill crown, £170.

Proof pennies are equally valuable: those of 1908 are priced at £185, and those of 1930 and 1939 at £140 and £120 respectively.

All the examples so far quoted are of sets and individual coins minted and issued at least several years ago, and in many cases during the last century. Most modern issues of proof coins are in fact just as likely to show the same high, long-term increases in value as those of the past and, perhaps more important still, even the short-term annual percentage rise in value can be far greater than the interest which would be received by the same amount of money invested in conventional securities.

For instance the Jersey Crown Set of 1966, consisting of two coins in an official Royal Mint case, cost £2·50 at the time of issue; by 1970 the same set was priced at £5. In other words, the value had risen by 100% in four years – 25% a year.

Two even more recent examples, this time from overseas, are the Bahamas proof set and the Jamaica decimal set of 1969.

The former, issued in July 1969, consists of nine coins, from 5 dollars to 1 cent, and cost, at the time of issue, £15. One year later it was priced at £20, a rise of over 33% in one year. The 1969 Jamaica decimal set consists of 6 coins from 1 dollar to 1 cent and cost £6·50. By 1970 it was priced at £8·50, a gain in value of some 30% per annum.

1970: even more outstanding has been the Proof 'Manx-cat' crown of the Isle of Man which was issued (mintage 15,000) at £5·00. Twelve months later the quoted price was £10·00, a rise of 100% in one year!

It is almost axiomatic that official proof issues, and particularly those of a strictly limited issue, will automatically increase in value at a higher annual percentage rate than any other normal investment.

Generally speaking, as fashions in collecting change and interest switches from one coinage to another, that which is newly popular gains rapidly in price, while that which is neglected tends to remain static in value or even temporarily to decline; this is particularly the case with coins in the lower grades.

However proof sets tend to ride smoothly over these temporary fluctuations because of their condition and their comparatively low mintages.

Country	Date	Mintage	No. of Coins	Price
New Zealand	1953	7,000	8	£32·00
Rhodesia and Nyasaland	1955	2,000	7	50·00
Cyprus	1955	2,000	5	30·00
Caribbean	1955	2,000	7	30·00
Guernsey	1956	1,050	6	45·00
Jersey	1957	1,050	4	30·00
Ceylon	1957	700	4	60·00
Ghana	1958	6,431	7	17·50
Nigeria	1959	1,031	6	50·00
Cyprus	1963	25,000	5	4·00
Sierra Leone	1964	10,000	6	6·50
Malawi	1964	10,000	4	3·50
Jersey	1964	10,000	4	7·50
New Zealand	1965	25,000	7	9·00
Uganda	1966	8,250	6	3·00
Trinidad and Tobago	1966	8,000	5	4·50
Tanzania	1966	5,500	4	3·75
Jersey	1966	15,000	4	3·75
Jersey (Crown Set)	1966	15,000	2	5·50
Guernsey	1966	10,000	4	8·00
Bahamas (Specimen Set)	1966	75,050	9	20·00
Western Samoa	1967	15,000	7	6·00
Singapore	1967	2,000	6	15·00
Guyana	1967	5,100	5	4·25
New Zealand	1968	40,000	6	3·75
Seychelles	1969	5,000	7	4·75
New Zealand	1969	50,000	7	3·75
Jamaica (1d. & ½d.)	1969	5,000	2	2·50
Jamaica (Decimal Set)	1969	8,530	6	8·50
Fiji	1969	10,000	6	3·75
Bahamas	1969	10,481	9	20·00
New Zealand	1970	20,000	7	4·00
Gambia	1970/66	1,500	7	10·50
Guernsey	1971	10,000	6	6·50

C

One of the best ways of ensuring that you learn of new official issues of proof coins and sets is to become a subscriber to *Spinks' Modern Coins and Banknotes*, which is published five times a year (with occasional supplements). This publication also gives the current prices, not only of new issues but of past ones from all over the world; furthermore, subscribers are almost guaranteed to be allocated at least one set or individual coin.

For those who would like to spread their net wider, modern Commonwealth Proof sets may be of interest.

Listed on page 57 are Commonwealth Proof sets issued by the Royal Mint, along with the mintage figures, the numbers of coins in each set and the 1970 purchase prices.

Some of the early issues are expensive, but others are still quite reasonable in price and will almost certainly increase.

Of the more recent issues in the above list the relatively small mintage issues would seem to have the most potential for price increase. Among these are the Singapore 1967, Guyana 1967, Jamaica (1d and ½d) 1969 and the Gambia 1970/66 sets.

CHAPTER ELEVEN

Year Type-Sets

An interesting, inexpensive, but nevertheless highly profitable long-term investment is the collection of year type-sets. Such a set consists of one coin of each denomination (except gold) issued during any one year; the coins, however, must be in either Brilliantly Uncirculated or Uncirculated condition. The growth viability of year type-sets applies not only to the coinage of Great Britain but to other countries of the world.

A 1966 year type-set of Great Britain (the last year in which shillings were minted) consists of eight coins: halfcrown, florin, Scottish shilling, English shilling, sixpence, threepence, penny and halfpenny.

If you had obtained one of each of these coins in Uncirculated condition straight from your bank, the total cost would have been 7s. 4½d. (37p).

At the time of writing (1971) the dealers' selling price for the set is £2. This means that in five years the value has increased by roughly 540%, or 108% per annum. Even supposing that you sell your set to a dealer and only receive 50% of catalogue value your 37p investment has still increased to £1 in five years, which is nearly 17% interest per year free of tax.

There is, moreover, nothing magical or special about the year 1966; type-sets of other years grow with similar rapidity.

In 1965, for example, when a year-set would include the Churchill Crown (which in itself has shown little or no increase in value, because approximately twenty million were issued) your investment of 62p (including case) by 1970 was selling at £3, which makes it a high-yield investment.

A 1963 set, again costing 37p, is now priced at £4·50 and one of 1962 at £5·25. These are enormous rates of growth compared with that which could be obtained by investing similar small sums in almost any other way.

If you had started collecting British year type-sets in 1953, at the beginning of the reign of Queen Elizabeth II, your maximum outlay in any one year would have been 12s. 4¾d. (62p) – farthings were minted during the years 1953–56 – and the minimum 5s. 4½d. (27p) (in 1967, when no shillings were issued), and your total outlay about £15·00. The present dealers' selling price for all these sets together is anywhere between £250 and £300.

Let us be pessimistic and assume that you only receive £120 for your collection; this would still amount to an overall gain of 800%, which is well over 50% per year – and remember too that every year you keep your sets they are growing in value.

Not very long ago a well-known London coin dealer offered for sale a complete collection of year type-sets from 1902 (the beginning of the reign of Edward VII) to 1967, but not including the crowns of George V, some of which are very valuable indeed. The price asked for the ten Edward VII sets was £1,500 (the cost of these sets at the time of issue being well under £10). The remainder of the collection, from the beginning of the reign of George V (first issue 1911) to 1967, a total of 57 years, was offered at £3,500.

To buy complete collections such as this is well beyond the means of all except the very wealthy collector, but in my view, it is a good investment either to buy complete sets for five or ten years back or to attempt to make up such sets from coins in your own collection plus any other odd ones you may have to buy as individual coins.

What of the future?

As there is irrefutable proof of the value growth of year type-sets of past years it is logical to assume that those of the future will show a similar growth in value, with, perhaps, the exception of 1967 because of the enormous number of coins which have been minted bearing that date. Nevertheless, in order to make a complete year type-set collection, coins of 1967 will have to be included.

The fact that we have now switched over to the decimal

currency system does not mean (as so many people seem to think) that these coins and whatever coins may be issued in the future will not grow in value in the way that those of previous years have done. Coins are coins, and so long as there are collectors those in excellent condition (as type-sets must be) are bound to rise in price, not only because they are complete sets but also because coins of past years in EF or Uncirculated condition will become more and more scarce and because as the population increases so will the number of collectors who desire these progressively scarcer coins.

Assuming that you start your year-type collection in 1968 (the year the first decimal coins appeared) you should have (or obtain) the following coins.

1968

Numismatically speaking this year is a peculiar one, in that all its non-decimal coins bear the date 1967 and some of the decimal sets issued by the Government are dated 1971. Nevertheless, I feel that they should be included since they were issued during 1968. The coins for the year therefore will be:

1. The complete set of Britain's first decimal coins, consisting of 10, 5, 2, 1 and ½ new pence issued (and it should be kept) in the official plastic wallet.

2. Decimal coins only. Ten new pence and five new pence dated 1968.

3. The combined set of pre-decimal and decimal coins. These are the halfcrown (1967), florin (1967), ten new pence (1968), five new pence (1968), sixpence (1967), threepence (1967), penny (1967) and halfpenny (1967).

1969

1. Decimal coins only. 10 new pence and 5 new pence.
2. As set 3 of 1968.

1970

1. Decimal coins only and 1970 Proof L.S.D. sets.
2. The combined set of decimal and pre-decimal coins. As the

halfpenny and the halfcrown were demonetized in 1969 these coins will be omitted, the set consisting of the florin (1967), ten new pence, five new pence, sixpence (1967), threepence (1967) and penny (1967).

1971

In 1972 the Royal Mint issued Proof sets of the old L.S.D. coins and dated 1970. These sets, which cost £3·00, were limited to three per person.

Foreign Year Type-sets

What has been said so far about the investment potential of British year type-sets applies, in general, to the coins of other countries as they affect collectors resident in those countries, particularly where there is a relatively large population with a proportionately large number of collectors (America is an excellent example). On the whole there is likely to be a greater demand in any individual country for the coins of that country, because of their ease of access and because they can be obtained at face value, whereas coins from overseas have normally to be obtained from dealers who, quite naturally, expect to make a profit and cover the extra expense of importation.

Nevertheless, year type-sets in Uncirculated condition of coins of any country are usually a safe investment, though the annual percentage gain is likely to be greater with the coins of one's own country.

CHAPTER TWELVE

Coin Type-sets

A popular and attractive type of collection is that composed of coins of a single denomination – halfcrowns, say, or pennies. However it would be financially out of the question for most average collectors to collect all the coins of one type issued, for example, during this century, or even during a whole reign – though it would be easy to start a future collection of such coins, for you can obtain them in Uncirculated condition at face value.

Let us consider as an example what would be involved in making a complete collection of halfcrowns, starting with the year 1901, when Edward VII came to the throne.

Halfcrowns were issued in his reign every year from 1902 to 1910, when his reign ended. Here are the current prices of these coins in EF condition:

1902	£18·50
1903	160·00
1904	120·00
1905	240·00
1906	32·00
1907	38·00
1908	55·00
1909	42·00
1910	26·00

Need I say more? The first nine years of the century have already cost £731·50 – and a George V halfcrown of 1925 could cost you another £75.

You may think that I have given an extreme case by selecting halfcrowns as an example, but suppose you collected pennies: 1919 H and 1919 KN pennies would cost £18 and £85 respectively; a 1949 brass threepence could cost you £50, a 1913 halfpenny £5 and even a farthing dated 1910 can cost more than £10.

An alternative form of collection which may be more suitable for the average collector would be a type collection of the coin in which you are specially interested. This consists of one coin of each type issued during the reign or period you have selected.

Look at the catalogue prices of pennies in E F condition for the first ten years of this century:

Victoria (Old Head)

| 1900 | £2·50 |
| 1901 | 1·25 |

Edward VII (only one type of penny was issued during his reign)

1902	£2·25
1903	3·50
1904	7·00
1905	6·00
1906	5·00
1907	3·00
1908	4·00
1909	7·00
1910	3·50

From these figures you will see that taking one of each type can cost you as little as £3·50 (coins dated 1901 and 1902) or as much as £9·50 (1900 and 1904 or 1909).

Thinking entirely of the average collector with very limited financial resources, I have listed on the following pages some suggested type collections of British coins, beginning with the reign of George V. In each collection I have selected the least expensive coins in VF and EF condition, and have ignored expensive variations such as the 1902 'Low-tide' penny and the more expensive H and KN pennies of 1918 and 1919. Similar collections can, of course, be made for any chosen period of time or particular reign. The prices quoted are those current at the time of writing and should be checked from Seaby's *Standard Catalogue of British Coins* when the collection is being made. (Asterisks indicate that no catalogue price is given.)

Halfcrown Type-set 1910–69

George V 1910–36	Year	VF	EF
First coinage 1911–19 (92·5% silver)	1916	£0·85	£4·00
Second coinage 1920–26 (debased, 50% silver)	1920–21	1·25	11·00
Third coinage 1926–27 (modified effigy)	1927	2·00	6·00
Fourth coinage 1927–35 (new designs)	1928	0·35	2·00
Posthumous coinage 1936 (issued after the death of the King)	1936	*	1·50
George VI 1936–52			
First coinage 1937–46 (50% silver)	1946	*	1·00
Second coinage 1947–48 (cupro nickel)	1948	*	0·50
Third coinage 1949–52 (IND. IMP. omitted)	1949	*	0·50
Elizabeth II 1952–)			
First coinage 1953	1953	*	0·50
Second coinage 1954–67 (BRITT. OMN. omitted)	1967	*	0·20

This gives you a total of ten coins, all of which can be in at least VF or perhaps even EF condition without breaking the bank; apart from being numismatically satisfying, such a collection has good potential value growth, and would cost only about £28 in EF condition.

My second example is a brass threepence type-set from 1937 (the first year of normal issue) to 1967, a period of thirty years but involving the collection of only four coins.

Brass Threepenny Piece Type-set 1937–67

George VI (1936–52)	Year	EF
First Issue 1937–48	1937	£0·60
Second Issue 1949–52 (IND. IMP. omitted)	1952	0·50
Elizabeth II (1953–)		
First Issue 1953	1953	0·50
Second Issue 1954–67 (BRITT. OMN. omitted)	1967	face value

Four coins only may at first sight seem not a very satisfying collection, but it is a *complete* type-set, whereas if you tried to collect a complete year-set of EF threepences you would be faced with the possibly insurmountable barrier of the coins of

1946, 1948, 1949, 1950, 1951 and 1958, which are catalogued as below:

Year	VF	EF
1946	£6·00	£35·00
1948	1·25	5·00
1949	10·00	50·00
1950	2·50	9·00
1951	3·25	20·00
1958	2·00	5·00
Total	25·00	124·00

Complete year-sets have high potential and are extremely satisfying but most of them are far beyond the means of the ordinary person.

My final example is a penny type-set from the beginning of the reign of Edward VII to the present day. I have again divided these into the various reigns, for guidance on Reign Sets, if you wish to start later. I have also left out expensive variations which are normally beyond the means of the average collector. The cheapest catalogued coin is given for each type.

Penny Type-set 1902–67

	Year	VF	EF
Edward VII (1901–10)			
One type-issue only 1902–10	1910	£1·25	£3·50
George V (1910–36)			
First issue 1911–26	1920–21	0·50	2·50
Modified effigy 1926–27	1927	0·75	3·00
Third issue (small head) 1928–36	1935	0·40	2·00
George VI (1936–52)			
First issue 1937–48	1937, 1947–48	0·20	0·75
Second issue 1949–51 (IND. IMP. omitted)	1949	0·22½	0·90
Elizabeth II (1953–)			
First issue	1953	1·00	2·00
Second issue 1961–67	1967	face value	face value
(Note: no pennies were issued from 1954–60. BRITT. OMN. omitted)			

This gives a penny type-set of eight coins at a maximum cost in EF condition of £14·65.

Though my examples are taken from British coins, the same principles apply to coins of all countries. Importantly, though such sets may be extremely expensive, it is very possible to pick on one which suits your pocket. And of course you can always amalgamate or expand existing sets to form larger and more comprehensive collections.

CHAPTER THIRTEEN

Thematic Collections

Thematic collections of coins can be both a fascinating pursuit and a means of widening one's numismatic horizons, for they compel one to include coins of many countries of the world.

A thematic collection consists of coins devoted to a particular subject or bearing designs of a similar nature. These can include such things as political events, sport, industrial occasions and engineering feats, exploration, music, composers and literary celebrities, famous statesmen, birds, flowers, animals and even romantic occasions.

On the following pages I give examples of ways in which coins can be included in such thematic collections as those mentioned above. As always, these coins should be obtained in at least Extremely Fine condition and, where possible, as Proof coins.

Political Themes

Many countries have struck special issues of coins to celebrate or commemorate their independence or other such events in their political history. Here are some examples; I have confined myself to post-World War II issues, as being comparatively easy to obtain.

Argentina

1 peso 1960   150th year of independence

Cameroon

50 francs 1960   Commemorating formation of independent state

Canada

1 dollar 1949	Commemorating the entry of Newfoundland into Canada as a Province
1 dollar 1964	Confederation commemorative coin

Czechoslovakia

50 korun 1947	Commemorating Slovak uprising, August 29th, 1944
100 korun 1948	Commemorating the thirtieth anniversary of separation from Austria
10 korun 1955	Tenth anniversary of liberation from Nazis, 1945
50 korun 1968	Fiftieth anniversary of republic and twentieth anniversary of People's Republic

Egypt

50 piastres 1956	Evacuation of the British

Finland

10 markkaa 1967	Fiftieth year of independence

Guernsey

10 shillings 1966	Norman conquest commemorative

Ireland

10 shillings 1966	Commemorating 1916 uprising

Israel

10 pounds (silver) 1968	20th anniversary of independence

Italy

500 lire 1961	Italian unification commemorative

Mexico

10 pesos 1960	Commemorating the revolutions of 1810 and 1910

South Africa

5 shillings 1960   50th anniversary of union

Sweden

5 kronor 1966   Commemorating reform of Parliament

Switzerland

5 francs 1948   Centenary of Swiss confederation

Zambia

5 shillings 1965   First anniversary of independence

Sport Commemoratives

As yet there are not many coins commemorating sporting events, but the practice of producing such coins appears to be on the increase; a start to what might provide a most interesting thematic collection with considerable investment potential can be made with the following modern coins.

Finland

500 markkaa silver   Olympic Games, 1952, Helsinki
  1951–52
10 markkaa   European Games 1971

Japan

100 and 1,000 yen   Olympic Games 1964, Tokyo
100 yen   Winter Olympic Games 1972

Mexico

25 pesos 1968   Olympic Games 1968, Mexico City

Austria

50 schilling 1964   Winter Olympics 1964

Jamaica

crown 1966   Eighth British Empire and Common-
                wealth Games 1966, Kingston,
                Jamaica

Thailand

1 baht 1966	Fifth Asian Games

Panama

5 balboas 1970	Central American and Caribbean Games

Germany

(not yet issued)	Olympic Games, 1972, Munich (1969–70–71–72)

Engineering and Industry

Many countries of the world have produced special coins to commemorate outstanding industrial occasions or feats of engineering. It is not often realized, for example, that the British Crown of 1951 was struck to commemorate a great commercial occasion, the Festival of Britain.

Some modern examples of this type of coin are as follow:

Belgium

50 francs 1958	Brussels World's Fair (Expo)

Egypt

1 pound and 5 pounds (gold) 1960	Aswan Dam commemorative
5, 10, 25 and 50 piastres 1964	Diversion of the Nile commemorative
5 piastres 1968	International fair
1 pound (silver) 1968	Aswan Dam

Germany (Federal Republic)

5 deutsche mark 1968	400th anniversary of the death of Johannes Gutenburg

Hungary

20 forint 1956	Szechenyi Bridge, Budapest

Israel

5 pounds (silver) 1962	Industrialization of the Nege

Mexico

5 pesos 1950   Inauguration of south-eastern railway

Portugal

20 escudos (silver)   Salazar Bridge commemorative
  1966

Exploration

Modern coins on this theme are not numerous but the coins
are almost invariably of extremely fine or striking design. Here
are examples:

Portugal

5, 10 and 20 escudos   500th anniversary of the death of
  1960   Henry the Navigator

Portuguese Guinea

50 centavos and 1   500th anniversary of the discovery of
  escudo 1946   the country

New Zealand

1 dollar 1969   Voyage of Captain Cook

Canada

1 dollar 1949   This coin has already been included in
                                 the Political list but as it shows the
                                 ship of John Cabot, the discoverer
                                 of Newfoundland, I have also
                                 included it here.

Music and Literature

Some examples of coins which will fit into this category are:

Austria

25 schilling 1955   Commemorating the State Theatre
25 schilling 1956   Bicentenary of the birth of Mozart
50 schilling 1967   Centenary of the Blue Danube Waltz

Bulgaria

2 and 5 leva (silver) and 10 and 20 leva (gold) 1963   1100th anniversary of Slavic alphabet

Czechoslovakia

10 korun 1968   Centenary of Prague National Theatre

Egypt

5 pounds (gold) 1968   1,400th anniversary of the Koran

Hungary

25 and 50 forint (silver) 1961   Liszt commemorative

25 and 50 forint (silver) 1961   Bartok commemorative

Italy

500 lire 1965   Dante commemorative

Personalities

Under this heading come a large number of men and women who have in their time made an impact in world affairs in a wide variety of ways, political, scientific, military and so on. A short selection of this type of coin is given below, but there are very many more.

Great Britain

crown 1965   Churchill commemorative

China (Nationalist)

5, 10, 50, 100 yuan (silver) 1965   Sun Yat Sen commemorative

1 yan 1966   80th birthday of Chiang Kai-shek

Colombia

20 centavos 1953   Simon Bolivar commemorative

Czechoslovakia

50 and 100 korun 70th birthday of Stalin
  1945

German Democratic Republic

20 marks 1968 Sesquicentennial of Karl Marx

India

50 paise 1964 Nehru commemorative

Israel

50 and 100 pounds 10th anniversary of death of Chaim
(gold) 1962 Weizman

Philippines

50 centavos and 1 General MacArthur commemorative
peso 1947

Poland

10 zlotych 1967 Marie Curie centennial

Southern Rhodesia

crown 1953 Commemoration of birth of Cecil
  Rhodes

United States of America

50 cents 1964 President Kennedy commemorative

Birds, Animals and Flowers

There is enormous scope for a most artistic and worthwhile collection of not-too-expensive coins under each of the above subjects. As any list of all these coins would take a complete book in itself, I have merely listed a few under each heading. Many more will be found described and illustrated in *A Catalogue of Modern World Coins* and *Current Coins of the World*, both by R. S. Yeoman.

BIRDS
Great Britain
farthing 1937–56   Wren

Irish Free State
penny 1928 onwards   Hen and chickens

Australia
10 cents 1966   Lyre bird

Bahamas
2 dollars 1966   Two flamingoes

Canada
1 dollar 1967   Flying goose

Chile
5 and 10 pesos and $\frac{1}{2}$, 1, 2, 5, 10} Flying condor
  centesimos 1956

Hungary
25, 50, 100 forint 1967   Peacock

Malawi
sixpence 1964   Cockerel

New Zealand
1 shilling 1953–65}
20 cents 1967   }   Kiwi

Rhodesia and Nyasaland
Florin 1955–57   Eagle

Tanzania
20 senti 1966   Ostrich

Zambia

1 shilling 1964 ⎫
1 shilling 1966 ⎪   Toucan
5 ngwee 1968 ⎬
10 ngwee 1968 ⎭

ANIMALS

Australia

A kangaroo appears on pennies and halfpennies; other coins bear pictures of a sheep, lizard and the duck-billed platypus.

Bahamas

Fishes, including a starfish and swordfish, are illustrated on the 1966 issue of the coinage.

Belgian Congo

On the issues from 1943–49 there is the picture of an elephant.

Canada

Some of the issues from 1937 onwards bear representation of a beaver and a moose, while the Confederation centenary commemorative coins (1967) show a hare, puma, prairie dog and a fish (in addition to the goose on the dollar).

Congo

10 francs (aluminium) 1965   Lion

Gambia

2 shillings 1966   Head of an ox
4 shillings 1966   Crocodile
8 shillings 1970   Hippopotamus

Guernsey

Threepence 1956 ⎫
10 new pence 1968⎬   Guernsey cow

Ireland (Eire)

The coinage of Eire shows a fish, bull, greyhound, hare and horse.

Italy

2 lire (1953–59)	Bee
5 lire 1951	Fish

Mauritius

Quarter and half-rupee 1950–51	Stag
Half-rupee 1965 onwards	

Norway

5 øre 1958	Moose
50 øre	Husky
1 krone coin	Horse

In addition to those already mentioned, the following countries also have animals on their current coinage: *Peru* (Alpaca), *Rhodesia* (buck), *Ruandi and Burundi* and *Sierra Leone* (lion), *South Africa* (springbok), *Tanzania* (rabbit and fish), *Tonga* (turtle) and the *United States* (bison).

Most of all the above-listed current coins can be obtained at very reasonable cost, except the $\frac{1}{4}$, $\frac{1}{2}$ and 1 golde of Sierra Leone (very large coins), all struck in gold to commemorate the 5th anniversary of independence; on the other hand, the $\frac{1}{2}$ cent of 1964 (fishes) and the 20 cents of the same year (a stylised lion) cost only a few shillings.

Flowers, Trees, Fruit

Though there are not so many coins bearing representations of flowers as those with animals, nevertheless a delightful and relatively inexpensive collection can be made on this theme. Here are some examples of such coins in current usage.

China

1 and 5 chio 1967	Orchid

Cyprus

50 mils 1963   Grapes

Denmark

25 øre 1966   Fir cones

Gambia

6 pence 1966   Ground nuts

Great Britain

sixpence and florin 1953   Rose, thistle, shamrock and leek
  onwards

Guatemala

50 centavos 1962   Orchid

Guernsey

4 and 8 doubles 1956–66 ⎫
5 new pence 1968   ⎬ Lilies

Iraq

5 and 10 fils 1967   Palm trees

Israel

25 pruta 1949 and 1954   Grapes

Italy

5 lire 1946–50   Grapes

Lebanon

A number of coins bear a representation of a Cedar tree

New Zealand

2 cents 1967   Native flowers

Nigeria

2 shillings, 1 shilling,   Native flowers
  sixpence and
  threepence 1959

Peru

5, 10, 25 centavos	Native flowers

Rhodesia

sixpence 1964	Native flowers

South Africa

10 and 20 cents 1965–69	Native flowers
50 cents 1965–69	Arum lily and native flowers

South Vietnam

10 and 20 su 1953	
50 su 1960	
1 dong 1960	
50 xu 1963	Native flowers or rice plants
1 dong 1964	
5 dong 1966	
10 dong 1964–68	

Uruguay

1, 5, 10 pesos 1968	Native flowers

Zambia

sixpence 1964	Native flowers

Romantic Themes

So far there have been few modern coins with romantic themes, but there is no reason to suppose that there will not be more. The following seven coins, well worth a place in any collection, are as yet relatively inexpensive and could form the basis of an interesting and potentially valuable investment.

Denmark

2 kroner 1958	18th birthday of Princess Margrethe
10 kroner 1967	Wedding of Princess Margrethe
5 kroner 1960	Silver Wedding of King Frederick I X and Queen Ingrid
5 kroner 1964	Wedding of Princess Anne-Marie
10 kroner 1968	Wedding of Princess Benedikte

Greece

30 drachmai 1964   Wedding of Constantine II to Princess
                    Anne-Marie of Denmark

Belgium

50 francs 1960   Wedding of King Baudouin to Princess
                    Fabiola

The coins described in this chapter are merely suggestions
for the formation of thematic collections; many more themes
are possible – ships, railways, military, religious, educational
and so on. Also, many coins will fit into several different
themes. It should not be hard to find a subject that coincides
with your own personal interests. But whatever theme you
choose, try always to obtain the coins in Extremely Fine or
better condition.

CHAPTER FOURTEEN

Silver Crowns and British Crown-size Coins

The silver crown made its first appearance in this country in 1551, during the reign of Edward VI (1547–53), though the name 'crown' was not new, for in the reign of Henry VIII there had been minted gold 'Crowns of the Rose' and 'Crowns of the Double Rose'.

To enumerate every one of these most satisfying and opulent-looking coins is beyond the scope of this book, and the prices of many of them are far beyond the pocket of the average collector.

Even in only Fine condition, for instance, a crown of Edward VI is catalogued at £85; while some of those of Charles I can cost well over £300. I propose, therefore, to concentrate mainly on the period from George III up to the Churchill crown of 1965 (which may well be the last crown to be minted in this country).

For those interested in the crowns of the earlier period, along with those of the present, I strongly recommend two books, *The Crown Pieces of Great Britain and the British Commonwealth* by H. W. A. Linecar and *English Proof and Pattern Crown-Size Pieces* by H. W. A. Linecar and A. G. Stone.

Crowns and Crown-size Coins of George III

For a period during the reign of George III Spanish dollars (eight reales) and later the same dollars countermarked with either an oval or octagonal stamp (see Chapter 20) circulated freely in this country. Some were also overstruck on the dollars, which had been planed flat, though traces of the original design can sometimes be seen below the new design. These Bank of England dollars were marked both FIVE SHILLINGS and DOLLAR on the reverse, along with the words BANK OF ENGLAND

and the date, 1804. This date remained constant, though they were struck until at least 1811. In VF condition they are catalogued at £20.

The first real crown of the reign was struck in 1818 and is notable for the brilliant St George and the Dragon designed for the reverse by the Italian designer Benedette Pistrucci, and which has been used on many of our gold coins and crowns ever since.

The crowns were struck in three years, 1818–20, but in the first two years there are two variations with different regnal years (year of reign) on the edge.

	F	VF	EF
1818 (Regnal date LVIII on edge)	£3·50	£10·00	£30·00
(Regnal date LIX)	3·75	11·00	37·50
1819 (Regnal date LIX)	3·00	8·50	30·00
(Regnal date LX)	3·25	10·00	40·00
1820 (Regnal date LX)	3·00	9·00	32·50

Crowns of George IV (1820–30)

There were three normal issues, 1821 and 1822 (two variations). There was also a special proof crown in 1826; in FDC condition this is catalogued at £300.

The issues of 1821 and 1822 are catalogued as follows:

	F	VF	EF
1821 (Regnal date on edge SECUNDO)	£3·00	£8·50	£45·00
1822 (Regnal date on edge SECUNDO)	5·00	12·00	70·00
(Regnal date on edge TERTIO)	4·50	10·00	60·00

Crowns of William IV (1830–37)

Only one crown was struck during this relatively short reign. This was the special proof issue of 1831 and is one of the most valuable coins of modern times, being catalogued at £750 in FDC condition.

Crown of Victoria (1837–1901)

The four types of crowns issued during Victoria's long reign are among the most interesting of modern times and one of them, the 'Gothic' crown (so called because of the Gothic script used in the legend), is considered by many numismatists to be among the most beautiful of all British coins.

The four types of crowns are the Young Head, the 'Gothic', the Jubilee Head and the Old Head.

Young Head Crowns

Young head crowns were issued in the years 1844, 1845 and 1847, though there was also a special proof striking in 1839 which in FDC condition is catalogued at £375.

The crowns are not often found in EF condition, though when they are they tend to be expensive, as is shown in the following catalogue extracts:

	F	VF	EF
1844	£5·00	£17·50	£85·00
1845	5·00	17·50	85·00
1847	6·00	20·00	90·00

The 'Gothic' Crown

This extremely beautiful and valuable crown was struck in 1847 (the date is in the legend in Gothic script: mdcccxlvii). It was probably not issued for general circulation. It is catalogued VF £60, EF £90 and FDC £130.

The Jubilee Head Crown

To commemorate the Golden Jubilee of Victoria's reign in 1887, a new design silver coinage was issued. On the obverse a somewhat stern-looking Queen is seen wearing a small crown perched precariously on top of her head.

These crowns are issued for general circulation from 1887 to 1892. They are not particularly valuable, as can be seen from the following catalogue prices:

	F	VF	EF
1887	£1·75	£4·00	£12·00
1888	3·50	10·00	25·00
1889	1·50	4·00	13·00
1890	2·00	5·00	16·00
1891	2·25	5·50	17·50
1892	2·25	7·00	20·00

Old Head Crowns

These were issued from 1893 to 1900. As Victoria was proclaimed Queen on 20 June, 1837 there are *two* regnal dates in the edge legend for each of the years of issue. A complete collection, therefore, of Old Head crowns would consist of sixteen coins, two for each year. They are catalogued as below:

Issue date	Regnal date	F	VF	FE
1893	LVI	£1·50	£7·00	£25·00
	LVII	4·50	20·00	50·00
1894	LVII	3·25	10·00	35·00
	LVIII	3·25	10·00	35·00
1895	LVIII	2·75	8·50	30·00
	LIX	2·75	8·50	30·00
1896	LIX	3·75	14·00	45·00
	LX	2·75	8·50	30·00
1897	LX	2·75	8·50	30·00
	LXI	1·75	6·50	25·00
1898	LXI	4·00	18·50	50·00
	LXII	3·25	10·00	35·00
1899	LXII	3·25	10·00	35·00
	LXIII	3·25	10·00	35·00
1900	LXIII	3·25	10·00	35·00
	LXIV	2·75	8·50	30·00

Crowns of Edward VII

Only one crown was issued during the relatively short reign of Edward VII, in 1902. It is catalogued £8 (F), £15 (VF), £32·50 (EF).

Crowns of George V

Contrary to previous practice, no crowns were issued at the beginning of the reign of George V.

However a proof crown was issued in 1927 (FDC £37·50) and in the years 1928–34, plus one specially designed for the King's Silver Jubilee in 1935.

The crowns of 1927–34 and 1936 bore the head of the king on the obverse, and on the reverse a somewhat involved design with a central crown surrounded by an ornate wreath of leaves, roses and thistles replacing the classical Pistrucci St George and the Dragon.

The issues of 1928–31 and 1933 are catalogued at approximately £25 (VF) and £45 (EF), while that of 1932 is valued at £32·50 (VF) and £65 (EF).

The really valuable crown, however, is that of 1934, when only 932 were issued; it is priced at £150 (VF) and £300 (EF).

The Crown of 1935

To commemorate the Silver Jubilee (25 years) of the reign of George V, the St George and the Dragon motif was reintroduced on the reverse, but instead of the beautiful Pistrucci design, one in the 'modern idiom' by Percy Metcalfe was used. This 'Wooden Horse' design was far from popular in many numismatic circles, and the coin has increased less in value than any of the others of the reign. At the time of writing the normal issue coin is catalogued at £2·50 (VF) and £5 (EF).

In addition to the 714,769 issues of the above crown, twenty-five special Jubilee crowns were made in gold and two thousand five hundred were struck in sterling silver. These last were distributed by ballot, the Mint having received far more orders than they could supply. They had an edge inscription in relief; on the normal coins it is incuse. They are catalogued at approximately £90 (FDC).

The Crowns of George VI (1936–52)

Two crowns only were struck during this reign, the first in 1937 to mark the introduction of the new coinage, and the second in 1951 (made of cupro-nickel) on the occasion of the Festival of Britain, the industrial exhibition held on the South Bank in London.

The 1937 Crown's reverse shows the royal arms with supporters and the legend FID: DEF: IND: IMP above and CROWN: 1937 below. It is catalogued at £4 (VF) and £8·50 (EF).

The 1951 Crown, which reverts to the famous Pistrucci reverse, has certain unusual points, bearing the date in ordinary numerals on the reverse and the same date on the edge in Roman figures. There is also the date 1851 on the edge (the date of the Victorian 'Great Exhibition'. By coincidence (or design?) the crown marked the 400th anniversary of the issue of the first silver crown of 1551 and, ironically, was the first British crown to be struck in cupro-nickel with no silver content at all. It is catalogued at £2·75 (EF) and £4 (Unc).

The Crowns of Elizabeth II (1952–   )

Three crowns have been issued so far during the reign of Elizabeth II; the first was in Coronation year, 1953, the second in 1960 and the third in 1965 (the Churchill Crown). Another one is planned for November 1972 to commemorate the Silver Wedding of Her Majesty, Queen Elizabeth II.

The 1953 Crown, considered by many to be a mixture of coin and medal, is interesting in that the monarch is shown on horseback, the first time since Charles I. The horse was modelled on Winston, the horse which the Queen then rode at the Trooping the Colour ceremony on Horse Guards Parade. From a coining viewpoint it was not a success, as many of the finer details (plainly seen in a proof specimen) are blurred on the normal issue of 5,962,621 coins. Catalogue values: £1 (EF), £1·75 (Unc).

In addition to proof coins issued in the 1953 sets, there are in existence some extremely rare proofs or patterns in which the raised part of the design is frosted while the field is highly polished, and also a very few – not more than two or three – examples of patterns in which the whole coin is very dull, having been struck from sand-blasted dies. These coins would bring extremely high prices if sold.

The 1960 crown was issued on the occasion of the British Trade Fair in New York. 1,024,038 coins were issued in this country and are catalogued £2·50 (EF) and £4 (Unc). A large number of the crowns were struck at the Mint from polished dies and sold at the exhibition site in New York in special blue plastic cases. When the exhibition closed all unsold coins were returned to the United Kingdom in bags; the cases, somewhat foolishly, were disposed of in America. These polished coins bring higher prices than the ordinary UK issues.

The Churchill crown of 1965, intended as a tribute to Sir

Winston Churchill, and the first British coin to show the portrait of a commoner since Cromwell's time, is considered by many to be numismatically and artistically not of a high standard. On the reverse is a low-relief portrait of Sir Winston dressed in his siren suit. It was designed by Oscar Nemon and, it is reported, was done in a hurry, which may account for its lack of success. It is nevertheless unfortunate that on this almost unique numismatic occasion every effort was not made to produce a coin of outstanding beauty, and even more so when, as it turns out, it may well be the last crown to be struck in this country.

Nearly 20,000,000 of these coins have been struck, which means that their rate of appreciation may well be negligible, for at the time of writing (1970) they can still be purchased through banks at their face value of five shillings (25p). However they are catalogued by Seaby at £0·50 in Unc condition.

The Double Florin of 1887–90

The Jubilee Head coinage of Victoria included a new – and short-lived – double florin which, strictly speaking, should not be included in this chapter, except that it is only fractionally smaller than a crown. It was intended to join the florin in a move towards a decimal currency.

Known familiarly as 'the Barmaids' Curse', because of the frequency with which these ladies were supposed to confuse it with the crown and give change for five shillings instead of four, it became so extremely unpopular both with them and the general public that it was minted for four years only. There are two normal variations; some coins of the issue of 1887 have a Roman I in the date, whereas others, plus all those of the other three years, have an Arabic 1.

The catalogue values are as below:

	F	VF	EF
1887 Roman I in date	£2·00	£3·50	£10·00
1887 Arabic 1 in date	2·00	3·25	8·00
1888	2·25	5·50	16·00
1889	2·25	4·00	12·50
1890	2·50	6·50	17·50

There are rare errors in some of the 1888 and 1889 coins, in which the second I in Victoria's name is an inverted 1 – i.e. 1. Examples would bring sums well in excess of those for the normal issues.

Collecting Crowns

To make a complete collection of every type of crown minted since 1551 would probably take a lifetime and cost a fortune. It is, however, perfectly possible over a period of time to make a collection of, say, types of crowns of the twentieth century (as distinct from one example of every crown issued).

This would involve collecting the following eight coins. I have put down the prices of the coins in Very Fine, Extremely Fine and, where catalogued, Uncirculated condition.

	VF	EF	UNC
Edward VII, 1902	£15·00	£32·50	
George V, 1933	18·50	37·50	
George V, 1935	2·50	5·00	
George VI, 1937	4·00	8·50	
George VI, 1951		2·75	4·00
Elizabeth II, 1953		1·00	1·75
Elizabeth II, 1960		2·50	4·00
Elizabeth II, 1965			0·50

The total cost is not small, but if it can be raised gradually over a year or two, I am convinced that the investment, plus the pleasure of making and owning such a collection, would pay handsome dividends over the next five to ten years.

Two less expensive but nevertheless still interesting collections would be the six crowns of the last thirty-five years (starting with the 1935 Silver Jubilee crown of George V) or even the crowns of Queen Elizabeth and her father, George VI (five coins). When collecting such recent coins, resist the temptation to save money by buying low-grade examples – their growth potential is low.

The condition of a coin. Three typical modern coins are illustrated above, and below is listed the kind of wear to be expected in EF examples.

Obverse of Elizabeth II penny: 1. Very slight additional shine round the entire rim of coin. 2. Slight blurring of hair lines on crown of head. 3. Slight shine on projecting leaf of the laurel chaplet. 4. Slight shine on lock of hair above forehead and on forehead from eyebrow upwards. 5. Slight shine on Queen's cheek. 6. Slight shine on tips of two ribbons. 7. Slight shine on left side, lower shoulder.

Reverse of Elizabeth II penny: 1. Slight additional shine round entire rim of coin. 2. Shine on Britannia's left hand. 3. Slight shine on Britannia's cheek. 4. Slight shine or blurring of folds of drapery over Britannia's right shoulder. 5. Slight shine on Britannia's right forearm and on the thumb and finger resting on shield. 6. Slight shine on draperies hanging from Britannia's left arm close to her left thigh. 7. Shine on draperies on Britannia's right knee and leg almost down to her right foot. 8. Slight shine on high points of draperies immediately to the right of the centre bar of shield. 9. Slight shine on tips of waves immediately above the exergue line.

Reverse of Elizabeth II florin: 1. Increased shine on the rim of the coin. 2. Blurring of the lines on the 'pods' beneath the heads of the five thistles. 3. Slight blurring of the lines forming the leaves of the three leeks. 4. Slight smoothing or blurring of the cross-hatched lines in the centre of the central Tudor rose.

Reverse of Elizabeth II sixpence: 1. Increased shine on rim. 2. Shine on the patterned 'pod' under the thistle head. 3. Smoothing of the tips of the outside petals of the Tudor rose. 4. Smoothing of the two large lower leaves of the leek. 5. Smoothing of the surface of the large shamrock.

The Parts of a Coin

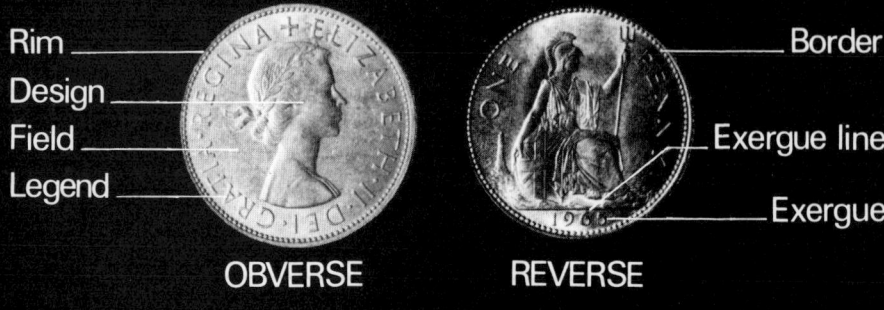

Rim   Border

Design

Field   Exergue line

Legend   Exergue

OBVERSE   **REVERSE**

Top, the parts of a coin.

Middle, the exceedingly rare dodecagonal nickel-brass threepence struck for Edward VIII, but never put into general circulation.

Bottom, the highly distinctive 'wooden horse' crown of George V 1935. Not universally well received, it is nevertheless a fine and easily collected piece.

Three Victorian crowns, showing the Gothic, Jubilee and Old Heads.

A complete proof set: George VI crown to farthing, 1951.

Two pages of 'Georges': all very elegant and well worth collecting. Top, the extremely valuable George III gold £5, of which only patterns exist; middle, a penny of George IV—the similar 1827 issue is uncommon, and can be worth as much as £200; bottom, the 1902 halfcrown of Edward VII is comparatively inexpensive—less than £20 in EF condition, but a 1905 example may be ten or more times the price.

Top, the very handsome halfcrown of George IV issued in 1823–4;
middle, a George IV sovereign, 1827—not as expensive as that of the
following year, which can top £1000, but much counterfeited—beware
of imitations; bottom, a sixpence of Edward VII, 1910—the kind of
not too expensive coin that sits nicely in a type-set.

Above, a maundy set—Victoria, 1875; middle, an 1845 farthing of
Victoria, young head, and an 1844 Victoria half farthing; bottom, a
fine 19th century copper token—a halfpenny struck for a coach
company.

CHAPTER FIFTEEN

Commonwealth Crown-size Coins

A most interesting and potentially excellent long-term coin investment would be a collection of modern crown-size coins of the British Commonwealth; it would be particularly good if confined to proofs.

Many of the earlier issues and some relatively modern ones of very limited mintages will be outside the financial range of the average collector; for instance, the New Zealand 'Waitangi' crown, which was issued in 1935 and had a mintage of only 1,128 (including 364 proof coins) could cost well over £200.

Those collectors who are interested in the earlier issues of Commonwealth crowns should read *The Crown Pieces of Great Britain and the Commonwealth* by H. W. A. Linecar, which is a most valuable book, copiously illustrated with excellent photographs and providing a wealth of detailed information on each coin.

The new or average-income collector would start by collecting Commonwealth crowns and crown-size coins issued since the beginning of the reign of Elizabeth II.

If crowns alone are collected, the collection is almost certain to end with the Isle of Man Manx Cat crown issued in November 1970. This coin is likely to be unique in that it is probably not only the last crown to be issued (due to decimalization in February 1971) but also the only known coin in numismatic history to feature a domestic cat as the main feature of the reverse design.

An alternative starting point for a collection which can be built up at minimum cost in the years ahead (for the coins can be purchased at issue prices) would be on the introduction of decimal coinage in common Commonwealth countries, a process

D

which began in 1966 in Australia. These decimal coins could, of course, make a 'collection within a collection' if a start were made with the accession of Elizabeth in 1952.

Among the coins within such a collection will be the following:

United Kingdom Crowns

1953 Coronation crown as described on p. 86.
1960 The crown struck on the occasion of the British Fair in New York, and described on p. 86.
1965 The Churchill crown, described on p. 86.

Jersey

Crown struck in 1966 to commemorate the 900th anniversary of the Norman Conquest, when the Channel Islands, originally part of the Duchy of Normandy, became a possession of the British Crown on the accession of William the Conqueror.

Isle of Man

In 1970 the Isle of Man struck its first crown and probably its last: described on p. 89.

Australia

50 cents, 1970. This coin has a diameter of 32 mm, whereas the normal crown size is 38 mm.

Bahamas

1966. The Bahamas issued, as part of the new decimal coinage, three large coins, five dollars, two dollars and one dollar. The five dollars bears on its reverse the arms of Bahama, the two dollars shows two flamingoes and the dollar a large conch shell.

Bermuda

Two crowns, 1959 and 1964. The first was struck to commemorate 350 years of association with British rule.

Canada

Over the period from 1952 to 1969 Canada has issued six types of dollars:
First Type, 1953–61 (except for 1958). The obverse has the Queen's head, designed by Mary Gillick; the reverse shows a two-man canoe.
Second Type, 1958 only. Struck to commemorate the centennial of the establishment of British Columbia as a Crown colony. Obverse: as first type. Reverse: totem pole, with legend CANADA. BRITISH COLUMBIA 1858–1958. In exergue, DOLLAR.
Third Type, 1964 only. To commemorate the centenary of the Confederation Conferences. The reverse has a central circle with a design of a rose, thistle, shamrock and fleur de lys surrounded by CHARLOTTE TOWN. QUEBEC.
Fourth Type, 1965–66. Obverse: a new portrait of Elizabeth II.
Fifth Type, 1967 only. Canadian centennial dollar. Reverse shows a goose in flight with the legend DOLLAR CANADA 1867–1967.
Sixth Type, 1968. As for fourth type, but struck in cupronickel.

Fiji Islands

1969, first issue of the new decimal coinage. Reverse shows the arms of Fiji with the legend ONE DOLLAR. The obverse legend is ELIZABETH II. FIJI 1969.

Gambia

Four shillings, 1966. Cupro-nickel; the country's first coinage as an independent member of the Commonwealth. Reverse: a crocodile, and 4 SHILLINGS (also in native script).
Eight shillings, 1970. Normal and Proof issues. Reverse: a hippopotamus with the legend 8 SHILLINGS (also in native script).

Gibraltar

Crown 1967–69. The 1967 issue was struck on the occasion of the 125th anniversary of Gibraltar's coinage. Normal issues struck in cupro-nickel, proofs in silver. Reverse shows a castle or citadel with a key suspended below, dividing the date 19/67. Legend: GIBRALTAR. ONE CROWN.

Jamaica

Crown 1966. Struck on the occasion of the Commonwealth Games held in Kingston, Jamaica. Cupro-nickel. Obverse: arms of Jamaica. Legend: JAMAICA. FIVE SHILLINGS. Reverse: a chain of twenty links inside which is a crown dividing the date and the legend VIII BRITISH EMPIRE AND COMMONWEALTH GAMES KINGSTON JAMAICA.

New Zealand

Crown 1953. Struck to commemorate the Coronation of Elizabeth II. Obverse: normal Mary Gillick head of the Queen. Reverse: Elizabeth II cypher surmounted by a crown, ornate pattern below. Legend: NEW ZEALAND CROWN + 1953.
One Dollar 1967. Cupro-nickel, struck to commemorate the first issue of the new decimal currency.
'Cook' Dollar 1969, struck to commemorate the bi-centenary of Captain Cook's famous voyage, during which he landed in New Zealand. The reverse shows a portrait of Captain Cook with his ship, HMS Endeavour.
Cook Island Dollar, 1970. Designed to commemorate the 1970 Royal visit to New Zealand, plus Captain Cook's voyage. Normal issue and Proof coins were struck.

Rhodesia

Crown 1953. Obverse: Mary Gillick portrait of Elizabeth II. Reverse: in a small circle, centrally above, a portrait of Cecil Rhodes with, below, three shields and CECIL RHODES. Legend: SOUTHERN RHODESIA. CROWN. 1953.

South Africa

As South Africa left the Commonwealth in May 1961, the only crowns within the specific period with which we are concerned are (1) that first struck in 1953 and issued until 1959 (these coins were specially polished but were not proofs) and (2) that struck in 1960.

Crown 1953–59. The obverse bears the head of Elizabeth II and the simple legend ELIZABETH II REGINA. The reverse shows a South African Springbok and the legend: SUID – AFRIKA – 1953 – SOUTH AFRICA * 5S *.

Crown 1960. Commemorates the Golden Jubilee of the South African Parliament (1910–60). Obverse: illustration of the South African Parliament Buildings with 1910 above and 1960 below. Legend: * UNITY IS STRENGTH * EENDRAG MAAK MAG. Reverse: arms of South Africa. Legend: + SOUTH AFRICA * 5S * SUID – AFRIKA – 1960.

To all the above could be added a 1957 5-rupee coin of Ceylon, a proof 10 shillings of Ghana (1958), a crown of Western Samoa dated 1967, a normal cupro-nickel and also a proof crown of Turks and Caicos, and a Guyana normal issue and proof crown of 1970.

CHAPTER SIXTEEN

Valuable Low-denomination Coins

By 1956 the long-lived farthing had overstayed its usefulness –
and become something of a nuisance to the housewife – and
in that year it was minted for the last time. Indeed, for many
years previously its only use was apparently to enable shopkeepers to use it as a sales bait by setting prices like 2/11¾ or
19/11¾. In 1960 it was demonetized and passed into numismatic history, along with such coins as angels, spur royals,
guineas and groats.

Yet few people realize that it was far from being the smallest-
value British coin minted in this country in relatively modern
times and that in the last one hundred and fifty years there
have also been half-, third- and even quarter-farthings.

These small-value coins, from the quarter-farthing to the
farthing, are not only fascinating numismatic items, well worth
collecting for themselves, but they also have potential growth
value. Most of them are still easily accessible, though some dates
and variations are so rare as to be extremely expensive and
beyond the means of the average collector; nevertheless very
satisfying type collections can be made, in the same way as is
suggested in Chapter Fifteen.

Farthings

As with other British coins, a very convenient date for starting
a collection of farthings is at the beginning of the reign of Queen
Victoria, in 1837, for many farthings of her reign are still in the
possession of older people or in 'that old box of coins that
grandfather gave me'.

The most valuable farthings of each type issued over the
period 1837–1956 are listed below. In each case the value is

given for coins in VF and EF condition; coins which are Un-circulated or Brilliant Uncirculated will be worth considerably more while those in the lower grades will be worth considerably less and coins which are extremely worn will be of little or no interest at all either to collectors or dealers.

Victoria (*1837–1901*)

Young Head (Copper) 1838–60. The coins of this period show the 'Young Head' of Queen Victoria on the obverse, with the date underneath, the legend reading VICTORIA DEI GRATIA. On the reverse is Britannia, with a design of a rose, thistle and shamrock in the exergue; the legend reads BRITANNIA: REG: FID: DEF:

	VF	EF
1844	£10·00	£25·00
1849	6·00	20·00
1851 (Variation with D of DEI over)	15·00	40·00
1852	6·00	18·00
1856 (Variation R of VICTORIA over E)	10·00	30·00

1860 (This coin is extremely rare and if found in VF or EF condition could be worth a considerable sum of money)

Young Head (Bronze Issue) 1860–95. Often referred to as 'Bun Head' coins.

Date	VF	EF
1863	£12·00	£30·00
1876 (H below date)	5·00	12·00
1895	5·00	12·00
Old Head 1895–1901		
1897 (Bright finish)	1·00	2·50

Edward VII (*1901–10*)

The farthings of this reign are on average considerably less expensive than those of Victoria, varying from £1·75 to £4 in EF condition.

The two most valuable issues of the reign are:

	VF	EF
1904	£1·50	£3·50
1910	1·75	4·00

George V (1910–36)

There are no really valuable farthings of this reign; the most expensive ones are catalogued as below:

	VF	EF
1911 (Blackened finish to prevent them being mistaken for gold sovereigns)	£0·50	£1·50
1915	0·75	2·50
1935		1·75

George VI (1936–52)

Most normal-issue farthings of this reign are catalogued at under 50p in EF condition; the catalogued exceptions are:

	EF
1938	£1·00
1940	0·75

Elizabeth II (1952–   )

There have been only four normal issues of farthings in the present reign. Their catalogue values are as below:

	EF	UNC
1953	£0·35	£0·50
1954 (BRIT: OMN omitted)		0·35
1955		0·25
1956 (Last date of issue)	0·60	1·00

The least expensive normal-issue farthing type-set (on catalogue values) from 1837 to 1956 would be, at the time of writing, as set out below, and would involve the collection of eleven coins. Prices are again given for coins in VF and EF condition.

Victoria Young Head (1860–95). Copper

	VF	EF
1853 (W.W. designer's initials raised and not incuse)	£0·75	£3·00

Victoria 'Bun Head' (1860–95). Bronze

	VF	EF
1891	0·50	1·25

Victoria 'Old Head' (1895–1901)

	VF	EF
1901 (Blackened finish)	0·20	1·00

Edward VII (1901–10)

	VF	EF
1909 (Blackened finish)	£0·50	£1·75

George V (1910–36)

	VF	EF
1916 (Blackened finish)	0·50	1·50
1919 (Bright finish)	0·25	0·75
1932 (Modified effigy with new reverse)		0·30

George VI (1936–52)

	Year	EF
First issue	1937–48	£0·25
(IND. IMP omitted)	1951	0·25

Elizabeth II (1952–   )

	Year	EF
First issue	1953	0·50
Second issue (BRIT. OMN. omitted)	1955	0·25

A twelfth coin can be added, that dated 1936. This is known as the 'Posthumous' issue of George V, because although he died in January of 1936, coins bearing his effigy continued to appear during the year as, owing to the abdication of Edward VIII, no new coins were issued for his brief reign. I have omitted this posthumous issue (VF £0·20, EF £0·60) as, apart from the date, it is identical with the 1926–35 issues.

Half-farthing

The half-farthing made its debut during the reign of George IV in 1828, when it was struck solely for use in Ceylon, but in 1842, during the reign of Victoria, it was also made current in the United Kingdom and remained so until it was demonetised in 1869.

The coins of George IV and William IV have Britannia on the reverse but on those of Victoria there is a crown and the words HALF FARTHING.

A complete year-set (one coin for each year of minting) from 1828 to 1868 in VF or better condition would be beyond the means of the average collector, for most of the pre-Victorian coins are very valuable:

George IV

	Year	VF	EF
	1828	£5·00	£10·00
(large date)	1830	6·00	15·00
(small date)	1830	12·00	20·00

William IV

	Year	VF	EF
	1837	8·00	20·00

On the other hand a complete normal-issue year collection of the Victorian coins in VF condition, though not cheap, is more within reach.

Victoria

Year	VF	EF
1839	£3·00	£7·00
1842	2·50	4·00
1843	0·60	1·00
1844	0·50	1·00
1847	2·00	4·50
1851	2·50	6·00
1852	2·50	7·00
1853	3·25	10·00
1854	3·25	10·00
1856	5·00	12·00

Third-farthings

The third-farthing was first issued under George IV in 1827. It was approximately the same size as the present-day half new penny.

A complete set of third-farthings, issued for use in Malta, would consist of twelve coins, beginning in 1827 and ending in 1913, during the reign of George V.

The issues of George IV (1827), William IV (1835) and the first of Victoria (1844) have Britannia on the reverse, but from 1866 onwards the reverse has a crown and, inside a wreath of leaves, the words ONE THIRD FARTHING and the date.

The normal-issue coins are:

George IV

	VF	EF
1827	£1·50	£3·50

William IV

	VF	EF
1835	1·10	2·25

Victoria

1844	£4·00	£10·00
1866	1·25	2·50
1868	1·25	2·00
1876	1·50	3·00
1878	1·25	2·50
1881	1·50	3·00
1884	1·25	2·25
1885	1·25	2·25

Edward VII

1902	0·50	1·25

George V

1913	0·50	1·25

There is a very valuable variation dated 1844 in which there are the letters RE instead of the normal REG (Regina). This coin is catalogued at £8 (F), £20 (VF) and £50 (EF).

Quarter-farthings

Like the half-farthing, the quarter-farthing was struck solely for issue in Ceylon, but its life was considerably shorter. There were only four normal issues, all Victorian, dated 1839, 1851, 1852 and 1853.

All these tiny 13-mm diameter coins show the 'young head' of Victoria on the obverse; on the reverse is a crown and the words QUARTER FARTHING along with the date.

Their present catalogue values are:

	VF	EF
1839	£3·25	£7·00
1851	4·75	13·00
1852	2·25	15·00
1853	5·00	14·00

It is obviously well-nigh impossible, unless you happen to be very wealthy, to make a complete year-collection of all these tiny coins; on the other hand you could collect one Very Fine or Extremely Fine coin of each denomination at not too great expense, if you select the most common years.

These would be:

	VF	EF
Half-farthing 1844	£0·50	£1·00
Third-farthing 1902	0·50	1·75
Quarter-farthing 1852	2·25	5·00

This gives a total outlay of £3·25 on VF and £7·75 in EF condition, which is perhaps not too great a price to pay for numismatic history. It also highlights the way in which the real spending value of money has decreased over the last century.

CHAPTER SEVENTEEN

Maundy Money

On Maundy Thursday, the last Thursday before Easter Day, at Westminster Abbey and in alternate years at other cathedrals, the Queen or her representative distributes to a selected number of old people a gift of Maundy Money, consisting of a number of small silver coins. They are of four denominations, from fourpence to a penny.

This ceremony derives from a similar practice of the early Christian Church, commemorating and emulating that great occasion when Christ bathed the feet of his disciples and commanded them to do likewise. Many hundreds of years ago it was a common practice for the actual washing of feet to be done and at the same time for clothes, food and money to be given to people selected for the ceremony. It is known that the first British King to have done this was Edward II (1307–27), who is said to have washed the feet of fifty poor men. Over the years the feet-washing was discontinued but the distribution of money continued.

The actual Maundy Money consists of as many pence as the age of the ruling monarch; thus, if the King or Queen is forty, each person selected receives four sets of the coins (each set totals ten pence); the following year the distribution would consist of four sets plus one penny, and the next year it would be four sets plus twopence, and so on. The coins are presented in a white bag.

Prior to the reign of Edward VII it was the practice of the Royal Mint to strike many more sets than would be required for the actual ceremony; these could be purchased by the general public and collectors through a bank. This, of course, to some extent not only reduced the importance of the gift to

the genuine recipients of the Maundy Money, but also depreci-
ated the market value of the sets. Edward VII ordered this
practice to be stopped and today only the number of coins
actually required for the recipients, plus some for the officials
taking part and some employees of the Royal Mint, are
produced.

Numismatically a complete year-collection of Maundy
Money could be of absorbing interest, but, as with so many
coins, well beyond the finances of the average collector; on the
other hand a satisfying type-set from the beginning of Victoria's
reign (1837) can be acquired over a period of time at not too
exorbitant a cost.

Details are given below of such a set; I have taken the least
expensive set of each type. The values are taken from *Seaby's
Standard Catalogue of British Coins.*

Maundy Type Set 1837–1967 (13 sets)

	EF	FDC
Victoria Young head (1838–87)		
1874, 1876–81, 1883–86	£10·00	£15·00
Victoria Jubilee head (1888–92)		
1889–92	14·00	17·50
Victoria Old head (1893–1901)		
1894–1901	8·00	10·00
Edward VII (1902–10)		
1903–08	8·00	10·00
George V First coinage (1911–20)		
1911–13, 1915–20	12·00	15·00
George V Second coinage (1921–27)		
1926	12·00	14·50
George V Fourth coinage (1928–35)		
1929–34	12·00	15·00
George V Posthumous coins (1936)		
1936		37·50
George VI First coinage (1937–46)		
1938–45		16·00

George VI Second coinage (1947–48)

	FDC
1947–48	£17·50

George VI Third coinage (1949–52)

1949–51	17·50

Elizabeth II First coinage (1953)

1953	70·00

Elizabeth II Second coinage (1954–69)

1962, 1964, 1966	20·00

It is interesting to note that the Maundy Sets are all 92·5% silver, except for the years 1921–46, when the silver was debased to 50%; yet in 1947, when the ordinary coinage was struck in cupro-nickel for the first time, the silver content of the Maundy coins was restored to 92·5%.

It is also of interest that, whereas the Maundy coins are strictly legal tender (though no one would be foolish enough to use them as such) and therefore 'normal' coinage, they are the only non-decimal coins to continue to bear the date of their issue from 1967 onwards.

The most valuable sets of each of the above types are as follows:

	Year	FDC
Victoria Young head	1841	£21·00
Victoria Jubilee head	1888	20·00
Victoria Old head	1893	11·00
Edward VII	1910	16·00
George V First coinage	1914	18·50
George V Second coinage	1921–22	16·00
George V Fourth coinage	1935	18·00
George VI First coinage	1937, 1946	17·50
George VI Second coinage	1947 48	17·50
George VI Third coinage	1952	21·00
Elizabeth II Second coinage	1969	45·00

Individual Maundy Coins

Many individual Maundy coins are available from a variety of sources, but often they are of lower grades than the coins found in the complete sets which are usually kept in small, rectangular boxes, each holding one set, provided by the Mint for the coins sold by the banks.

It is possible, of course, to build up sets from these individual coins at a slightly lower cost than that of the complete sets, but the labour and time involved in so doing can be considerable, and the quality of the complete built-up set may not be so even or so high.

At the time of writing, the minimum catalogue prices of these individual coins are:

Victoria Young head (1838–87)

	EF	FDC
Fourpence	£2·00	£3·00
Threepence	6·00	8·00
Twopence	1·50	2·50
Penny	1·25	2·00

Victoria Jubilee head (1888–92)

	EF	FDC
Fourpence	2·00	2·50
Threepence	6·00	9·00
Twopence	1·75	2·25
Penny	1·50	2·00

Victoria Old head (1893–1901)

	EF	FDC
Fourpence	1·25	1·75
Threepence	4·00	5·00
Twopence	1·25	1·50
Penny	1·25	1·50

Edward VII (1902–10)

	EF	FDC
Fourpence	1·25	1·75
Threepence	3·50	4·50
Twopence	1·25	1·75
Penny	1·25	1·75

George V, First coinage (1911–20)

	EF	FDC
Fourpence	1·50	2·50
Threepence	4·00	6·00
Twopence	1·50	2·00
Penny	1·75	2·50

George V Second coinage (1921–27)

	EF	FDC
Fourpence	2·00	3·00
Threepence	4·50	6·00
Twopence	2·00	3·00
Penny	2·25	3·00

George V Third coinage (1928–35)

	EF	FDC
Fourpence	2·00	3·00
Threepence	4·50	6·00
Twopence	1·75	2·50
Penny	2·00	3·00

George VI First coinage (1937–46)	*FDC*
Fourpence	£3·00
Threepence	3·00
Twopence	3·00
Penny	4·00

George VI Second coinage (1947–48)	
Fourpence	3·50
Threepence	4·00
Twopence	3·50
Penny	5·00

George VI Third coinage (1949–52)	
Fourpence	3·50
Threepence	3·50
Twopence	3·50
Penny	4·00

Elizabeth II, first coinage (1953)	
Fourpence	20·00
Threepence	20·00
Twopence	20·00
Penny	20·00

Elizabeth II Second coinage (1954–69)	
Fourpence	6·00
Threepence	6·00
Twopence	6·00
Penny	6·00

CHAPTER EIGHTEEN

Coins Worth a Fortune

Many coins are worth considerable sums of money and most of these can be found listed in catalogues with a definite price set by the side of them. For instance, a sovereign of George IV dated 1828 is catalogued at £300 in Fine condition, £600 if Very Fine and £1,250 if Extremely Fine; an Uncirculated specimen, therefore, could be worth at least £1,500. A Proof Crown of William IV dated 1831 in FDC condition is catalogued at £750, but even a penny of George IV dated 1827 in only EF condition could cost you £200.

Yet these most expensive coins are relatively cheap compared with some modern coins ('modern' being, numismatically, anything from the beginning of the reign of Victoria onwards) which when you look them up in a catalogue are not priced; instead, you will find words such as 'Very Rare' or 'Extremely Rare' or even '? exists'.

In *The English Silver Coinage from 1649* by H. A. Seaby and P. A. Rayner, twelve degrees of rarity are suggested:

R^7 Only one or two examples known
R^6 Three or four examples known
R^5 Five to ten examples known
R^4 Eleven to twenty examples known
R^3 Extremely rare
R^2 Very rare
S   Scarce
N   Normal, neither scarce nor common
C   Common
C_2 Very common
C_3 Extremely common

Taking examples from both ends of the scale, the almost fabulous 1954 penny (only one example known) would be classed as R⁷, the 1933 pennies would be R⁵, but the 1965 Churchill Crown is C_3, as are all coins dated 1967.

The locations of the Extremely Rare (or rarer) coins are usually known to expert or professional numismatists but occasionally a hitherto unknown coin appears out of the blue, often spotted in someone's change by a wide-awake numismatist. Such has happened at least twice in recent years: in the first case a man in Essex discovered in his pocket a 1952 halfcrown which was subsequently sold for over £1,000; and in 1969 a 1933 penny turned up in a collector's change. It was sold for £3,000 and the Mint subsequently stated that eight 1933 pennies were struck and not the six that were officially recorded. Since then there have been reports that two or three more such pennies have been found; if the reports are true other examples of this coin may appear in the future.

All of which proves the value of always inspecting every coin in your pocket and always keeping an eye open in junk-shops. You may never find an extremely rare coin, but some people have done so and others will in the future. Since decimalization a lot of scarce modern coins have been withdrawn from circulation, but there are plenty around still.

Listed below are all the British coins since 1837 which are identified as Rare or Extremely Rare or are catalogued at £150 or more in *Seaby's Standard Catalogue of British Coins*.

Gold Coins

Victoria

Five pounds, 1839. 'Una and the Lion.' Proof only. £1,000.
Sovereign, 1841. £450.
Sovereign, 1875. M below wreath for Melbourne Mint. Rare. No value stated.
Sovereign, 1879. EF £150.
Five pounds, 1893. Old Head. EF £155.

Edward VII

Sovereign, 1908. C on ground for Ottawa (Canada) Mint. VF £225, EF 285.

George V

Five pounds, 1911. Proof only. FDC £200.

Sovereign, 1917. Stated to be extremely rare. No value stated. Forgeries are known to exist.

Sovereign, 1913. C on ground for Ottawa Mint. VF £200, EF £250.

Sovereign, 1916. C on ground. Extremely rare.

Sovereigns, 1920, 1921, 1922, 1927. M on ground for Melbourne Mint. Each of these dates is classed '? exists'.

Sovereigns, 1924, 1928. M on ground. Very rare.

Sovereigns, 1930, 1931. Small Head. M on ground. Very rare.

Sovereigns, 1920, 1922, 1923, 1924. S on ground for Sydney Mint. Extremely rare.

Sovereign, 1924. 'SA' on ground for Pretoria (South Africa) Mint. Extremely rare.

Half-Sovereign, 1918. P on ground for Perth Mint. Extremely rare.

George VI

Five pounds, 1937. Proof only. FDC £160.

Elizabeth II

Proof five pounds, two pounds, sovereign and half-sovereign were struck in 1953 but none was issued for collectors.

Silver Coins

Victoria

Crown, 1839. Young Head. Proof only. FDC £375.

Halfcrown, 1839. Young Head. EF £250.

Halfcrown, 1848. Young Head. EF £120.

Florin, 1851. 'Gothic' type. mdcccli. VF £175, EF £300.

Florin, 1854. 'Gothic' type. mdcccliv. EF £175.

Sixpence, 1893. Jubilee Head. EF £150.

Edward VII

Halfcrown, 1903. EF £160.

Halfcrown, 1904. EF £120.

Halfcrown, 1905. EF £240.

George V
Crown, 1934. VF £175, EF £300.

George VI
Halfcrown, 1952. Extremely rare.

Copper, Bronze and Brass Coins
Catalogue values taken from *British Copper Coins and their Values, 1969–70*, edited by P. J. Seaby and Monica Bussell.

COPPER COINS
Victoria
Penny, 1849. Young head, copper. EF £150.
Penny, 1853. Young head, copper. Bronzed Proof. Reverse inverted. £150.
Penny, 1856. Young head, copper. Proof. £200.
Penny, 1858. Young head, copper. 8 of date over 3. EF £150.
Penny, 1860. Young head, copper. 60 of date over 59. EF £200.
Halfpenny, 1860. Young head, copper. Extremely rare.
Farthing, 1860. Young head, copper. Extremely rare.

BRONZE COINS
Victoria
Penny, 1861. Heavy Flan (170 grs.) EF £200.
Penny, 1865. 5 of date over 3. EF £150.
Penny, 1869. EF £200.
Penny, 1875. Proof in cupro-nickel. EF £150.
Penny, 1877. Proof in cupro nickel. EF £175.
Penny, 1881. Proof with heraldically coloured shield. EF £150.
Farthing, 1877. Proof, late striking. EF £300.

George V
Penny, 1933. 'Highest rarity', not issued for circulation.

Edward VIII
Threepence, 1937. Brass, dodecagonal. 'Exceedingly rare'.

Elizabeth II

Penny, 1954. Only one known to exist, valued at several thousand pounds.

In some years there were no official issues for general circulation of certain denominations of coins, and therefore such coins are officially unobtainable by the collector or dealer.

Two classical examples of this are the 1933 penny and the 1937 brass threepence bearing the head of Edward VIII. None of the latter were officially struck for circulation, yet there are a few in existence (the number is not known) and there is always the possibility that some will turn up at some time in the future.

There may therefore be coins in existence which 'officially' don't exist. (I have heard, for example, a report of a George V penny dated 1910), but all such coins should be viewed with the greatest suspicion, though once in a while a miracle does happen.

Years in which there have been no normal issues of UK silver, copper, bronze or brass coins, 1800–1967

Halfcrown 1800–15, 1822, 1827–28, 1830, 1832–33, 1838, 1847, 1851–67, 1869–73

Florin (First introduced for general circulation in 1849, though proofs were struck in 1848) 1850–51, 1861, 1882, 1934, 1952

Shilling 1800–15, 1822, 1828, 1830, 1832–33, 1952, 1967

Sixpence 1800–15, 1822–23, 1830, 1832–33, 1847

Threepence (silver). Last minted in 1944. 1800–33, 1847–48, 1852, 1869, 1923–24, 1929

Threepence (brass). First issued for general circulation bearing the head of George VI in 1937. 1947

Penny 1800–5, 1808–24, 1828–30, 1832–33, 1835–36, 1838, 1840, 1842, 1850, 1923–25, 1933, 1941–43, 1952, 1954–60

Halfpenny 1800–5, 1808–24, 1828–30, 1832–33, 1835–36, 1840, 1842, 1949–50, 1961

Farthing. Last minted in 1956. 1800–5, 1808–20, 1824, 1832–33, 1870–71, 1889, 1957–67

CHAPTER NINETEEN

Freaks and Mis-strikes

Errors in the printing of postage stamps can lead to an increase in their values, in certain cases astronomically, but this is not the case with coins. The reason for this is essentially simple. Numismatists look for perfection in coins, and any which are not in this condition are technically 'mutilated' (or worn) and of little interest except to the very few collectors who specialize in collecting freaks and mis-strikes. There are of course certain exceptions to this rule (which I will explain later) where errors or variations can lead to an enormous rise in value.

'Freak' Coins

Over the last few years I have seen many freak coins such as double-headed or double-tailed pennies and halfpennies, coins which are normal on one side and blank on the other, coins which have segments missing, one with a loose 'veil' hanging down from the back of the Queen's head, and another showing George V apparently smoking a large cigar.

Double-faced Coins

Double-headed or double-tailed coins *could* be genuine Mint errors but almost invariably they are fakes, often produced by superb craftsmen, either as exercises of their mechanical ingenuity or with intent to deceive. I am inclined to think that the former is the case, for so many of these coins are found in general circulation. If they had been produced for some dishonest or nefarious purpose, they would not normally be allowed to slip into change.

There are two main methods of producing such coins. The first is to slice two identically-dated coins in half edgeways, producing four half-thickness 'coins', all of them blank on one side. The two heads are then glued together, as are the two tails, producing both a double-headed and a double-tailed coin. Alternatively, two identically dated coins are ground down to half-thickness on the tails side and then the blank faces are glued together, giving an apparently double-headed coin.

The gluing of the coin is generally expertly done but even so the join can almost invariably be discovered by examining the edge of the coin under a powerful magnifying glass. This is particularly the case with smooth-edged coins such as pennies, halfpennies and the new 50p coin. Coins which have milled or grained edges are sometimes more difficult to detect if the ridges of the milling have been expertly lined up.

The second method of production is more complex and calls for consummate mechanical skill if an apparently genuine coin is to be produced. Again, two identical coins are needed – two 1967 pennies, say. On the first penny one side is cut out up to the rim so that this side becomes, in effect, a vertical-sided shallow dish. The second coin is then taken, the rim is ground off and the reverse ground down until it is almost, but not quite, the same thickness as the depth to which the first coin has been hollowed out; this bronze 'cork' or 'plug' is then dropped into the depression in the first coin and glued into position to produce a 'double-headed penny'.

If this is expertly done it is sometimes extremely difficult to detect, even with a magnifying glass, the hairline crack along the circumference of the coin.

However, it is *generally* safe to assume that any double-sided coin is a fake and one should always suspect that such is the case and send the coin to the Royal Mint for their microscopic examination and opinion. (Foreign examples should of course be sent to the Mint of the country concerned.)

These double-sided coins are interesting – and amusing – examples of mechanical skill, but have little or no numismatic value whatsoever. They are worth exactly what some collector of the curious is prepared to pay for them – and no more.

One-sided or Uni-faced Coins

As with double-faced coins, uni-faced coins – those with one side in quite normal condition and the other absolutely blank – could be genuine Mint errors (which can be verified by sending them for inspection as suggested above) but more often than not they are artificially produced.

If the blank side of the coin is absolutely smooth with no rim it is almost 100% certain to be a fake; even if it has a rim it should still be regarded as suspect until proved otherwise.

In the north of England in particular, a large number of one-sided coins have been in circulation, on whose smooth face there have been stamped or engraved slogans eulogising the particular merits of football teams and their chances (or certainty) of winning either the League Championship or the FA Cup. Numismatically, such examples of enthusiasm or propaganda are absolutely worthless.

Mint Errors

In spite of every precaution and, nowadays, the use of electronic production methods, errors can, and still do, occur during the minting and distribution of our coinage. This is not altogether surprising in view of the colossal numbers of coins which are struck each year. For instance in 1966 some 165,739,200 pennies, 53,160,000 threepences, 175,676,000 sixpences and 83,999,000 florins, plus other coins, were issued by the Royal Mint.

All these coins are subject to human inspection and no matter how highly trained and experienced these inspectors may be, it is inevitable that some coins, badly struck, or struck on previously damaged or imperfect blanks, are bound to pass their close scrutiny.

Of the three examples of mis-strikings given at the beginning of this chapter, the first two, the missing segment and the loose veil, were almost certainly due to faulty blanks which were not discovered prior to striking. The third, the cigar, was most likely caused by some foreign matter, such as a tiny piece of grit or even a drop of oil, either on the blank or on the die itself; even the tiniest particle can cause quite obvious imperfections on the surface of the coin because of the enormous pressures involved in the striking process.

These mis-strikes have very little effect upon the value of the coin concerned, for the collectors of such numismatic curiosities are very limited in number. Occasionally such collectors advertise in the Coins and Medals section of the weekly journal *Exchange and Mart* offering reasonable prices for the coins.

One type of mis-strike, however, which is of numismatic interest and can be worth considerably more than face value, is that known as a brockage.

Brockages

One side of a brockage, say the obverse, is in normal relief, but on the reverse side the obverse design is repeated but is incuse (hollow or cut-in). The reason for this condition is as follows.

Until a coin is struck it is essentially a blank circular piece of metal (gold, silver or bronze, or cupro-nickel). For striking, it rests on a die with the reverse side engraved upon it. Above it is a die in which is engraved the obverse design. The upper die comes down with great force upon the blank, so that the reverse is stamped upon the lower face of the blank and the obverse on the upper face. As the obverse die rises to get in position for the next striking, the newly impressed coin is ejected automatically and a new blank slides into place for the next blow of the die.

But it *can* happen, if very rarely, that the coin is not ejected, and the new blank slides in on top of it. This means that the obverse of the non-ejected coin has become, in effect, the lower die. Thus, when the real obverse die comes down again, the new blank receives the correct relief obverse impression on the upper face, and the *same* impression on the lower face, but hollowed out instead of in relief.

Brockages are quite rare, genuine Mint mis-strikes, and are sought after by many collectors as numismatic rarities and curiosities. Thus, their values are increased, though still not to the same extent as would be the case with a misprinted stamp.

CHAPTER TWENTY

Valuable Mutilations

As has been pointed out in the previous chapter, freak coins, mis-strikes and mutilations rarely increase the potential value of a coin, and more often than not decrease it; rare-dated gold coins which have chain attachments for pendants, or have been made into brooches by having a pin brazed on to them or have holes drilled in them for use on charm bracelets are, numismatically speaking, virtually worthless.

Yet there are at least three coins which have been *officially* mutilated, and are valuable or even extremely valuable indeed; two of them are rare but the third can still be discovered in antique shops and attics.

All three are based on or made from that most romantic Treasure Island coin, the Spanish Piece of Eight or, to give it its correct title, the Eight Reales (also known as a Spanish dollar).

Towards the end of the eighteenth century and during the early years of the nineteenth century there was a great shortage of regal silver currency both in England and in the British settlements and colonies overseas. At the same time, however, Spain was mining vast quantities of the metal in Mexico and her other American colonies, such as Peru, Bolivia and Chile, minting it into eight reales and smaller coins and shipping most of them back to Spain. These coins circulated and were accepted almost as official coinage in many parts of the world, including England. Technically speaking they were illegal in this country, but the government at first turned a blind eye to this practice and later, bowing to the economic inevitable, legalised the coins by counterstamping them.

Some of them also came from Spanish treasure ships captured

by the British Navy on their way to Spain. The silver coins then became Government property officially.

Countermarked Spanish Dollars and Half-dollars

In 1797 the British Government legalised the previously illegally circulating Spanish eight-reale pieces by counterstamping the obverse with the head of George III in a small oval. This was stamped on the neck of the portrait of Charles IV of Spain. The puncheon used was that employed by the Assay Master at Goldsmiths Hall for stamping the duty mark on silver plate assayed after 1785. The dollars were then made current at 4s. 9d., and gave rise to the saying 'two kings' heads not worth a crown'. Owing to the quantity of false dollars circulating, early in 1804 the stamp was changed, the King's head being larger and in an octagon. The punch used for the head was that for the Maundy penny. (*The English Silver Coinage from 1649*, H. A. Seaby and P. A. Rayner.)

A similar treatment was meted out to the Spanish half-dollar or four reales.

The catalogue values of these coins are as below:

Dollar with oval countermark VF £35·00.
Dollar with octagonal countermark VF £70·00.
Half-dollar with oval countermark. VF £32·50.
Half-dollar with octagonal countermark. Price not quoted but possibly about £70·00.

The 'Holey' Dollars of Australia and Canada

A much more drastic mutilation of the Spanish dollar was carried out in New South Wales (Australia) and Prince Edward Island (Canada), in that circular discs were cut out from the centres of the coins, leaving a 'coin' with the appearance of a large washer, hence the term 'holey' dollars.

Australia

Spanish dollars were circulating in New South Wales in the early part of the nineteenth century and were used as crowns. To discourage the export of the coins for their silver-bullion value, in 1814 the New South Wales Government mutilated £10,000 worth of the coins.

Circular discs, eleven-sixteenths of an inch in diameter, were cut from the centre of each coin, which still retained the original Spanish design. Around the inner rim of the obverse of the silver washer that remained were stamped the words NEW SOUTH WALES with the date 1813 (*not* 1814, the actual year of mutilation) diametrically opposite. On the inner rim of the reverse were the words FIVE SHILLINGS with two sprays of leaves opposite.

The cut-out central discs (known as 'dumps') had their original designs obliterated and a crown struck centrally on the obverse, with the words NEW SOUTH WALES round the rim above, and the date 1813 below; on the reverse, centrally in two horizontal lines, were the words FIFTEEN PENCE.

From the original £10,000 worth of dollars a total of just over 39,900 pairs of Holey Dollars and dumps were issued and remained in circulation for about sixteen years.

The approximate 1970 catalogue values of these coins in about Fine condition are:

Fifteen pence, 1813 (Dumps) £20–25+.
Five shillings, 1813 (Holey dollar) £125–150+.

The Canadian Holey Dollar

A somewhat similar situation to that in New South Wales arose on Prince Edward Island, Canada, in the early 1800s. Though Canada's official coinage was based on British sterling, the Spanish dollar circulated freely and was usually rated at five shillings. In some areas, however, the value was greater, and merchants shipped all they could obtain for exchange at the higher rate, with the result that Prince Edward Island began to run short of money. The Governor of the Island hit upon (or copied?) the Australian solution, being of the opinion that mutilated coins would be unacceptable anywhere else.

Consequently, he took and perforated 1,000 Spanish Dollars for use on the Island. The rings (or Holey dollars) were countermarked to pass for five shillings and the centres (which did not have their original design removed) for one shilling.

The coinage, however, did not circulate for more than about a year, after which it had to be withdrawn owing to the appearance of forgeries.

Because of the low mintage of the genuine Holey Dollars, these coins are rare and have become very valuable collectors' pieces, the dollar being catalogued at as much as £500 even in only Fair condition.

CHAPTER TWENTY-ONE

Variations

As is pointed out in Chapter Twenty-two, freak coins do not ordinarily gain in value like faulty stamps. There are, however, a number of coins in which minor differences in their design or striking add substantially to their values.

Take, for example, the Victoria young head penny of 1858. The catalogue entry for this coin reads as below:

	F	VF	EF
1858	£0·75	£1·50	£5·00
Smaller date	1·50	7·00	20·00
8 of date over 3	—	60·00	150·00
8 of date over 7	1·00	3·00	18·00
Without WW	0·52½	2·25	10·00

Similarly, the entry for the bronze Victoria penny of 1865 is:

	F	VF	EF
1865	£1·25	£5·00	£15·00
5 of date over 3	5·00	45·00	150·00

Consider also the catalogue entries for a George V penny of 1919.

	F	VF	EF
1919	£0·20	£0·60	£3·00
H in exergue	0·75	8·00	25·00
KN in exergue	1·12½	25·00	85·00

And one further example, another penny, this time that of 1926.

	F	VF	EF
1926	£0·30	£2·50	£10·00
Modified effigy	2·25	25·00	85·00

As I said in Chapter Two, the making of dies for striking coins is a very skilled and expensive process. During any one year a number of these dies are needed, particularly when there is a large striking of coins, but it may well happen – and often did – that at the end of the year one or more dies are in excellent condition and quite suitable for striking further coins. Sometimes instead of being destroyed (as was normally the case) they were put on one side for further use.

Later on these dies would be used to strike coins of a later year, but before this could be done the existing date had to be altered by cutting in the new date (generally only the last figure) over it. Even though this cutting was done most skilfully, more often than not slight traces of the old date were not completely obliterated on the die, and when the new coin is inspected under a powerful magnifying glass some traces of the last figure of the old date can still be seen.

Thus in the first-quoted example the variation '8 of date over 3' means that a die used originally to strike coins dated 1853, was re-cut to change the 3 to an 8, but traces of the original figure are still visible on the new coins. Similarly a die used to strike coins dated 1857 was re-cut for 1858, but traces of the original 7 are still visible.

In the second example the 1865 penny, a die of 1863 has obviously been used by cutting a 5 over the 3.

It must be remembered, however, that it is not the variations themselves which make the coins valuable *but their relative scarcity*. Obviously many dies must have been used to strike all the pennies minted in 1858 (1,599,040 of them), but only a very small proportion of them were struck using the altered dies; and this automatically increases their values.

H and KN Pennies

At various times over the last hundred years or more the Royal Mint has been hard pressed to produce the large numbers of small-value coins required to meet specific emergencies and has had to resort to help from outside commercial firms (under Mint supervision) to overcome the potential shortages.

In 1860, for instance, when the copper coinage was replaced by bronze, the change had to be made so quickly that the demands on the Mint were beyond their capacity and contracts had to be arranged for much of the new coinage to be produced by two Birmingham firms, Boulton and Watt and Ralph Heaton and Sons, who between them struck about 1,800 tons of the new bronze coins.

In 1874 (and on other occasions) the coining of part or all of the bronze coinage was again done by Heaton's; for instance, all 1874 farthings and all three denominations of 1876 and 1882 were struck by them. From 1874 onwards, all coins so struck bear a small H, either under or to the left of the date in the exergue.

In 1911, the introduction of the National Insurance Act created such a heavy demand for both silver and bronze coins that resort again had to be made to outside firms, this time, the Mint, Birmingham (who had succeeded Ralph Heaton and Sons in 1889), and the Kings Norton Metal Co. Ltd. The Mint, Birmingham, struck some of the 1912-dated coins (still marked with H) and also, along with the Kings Norton Metal Company Ltd, provided bronze blanks for pennies, halfpennies and farthings. In 1918 and 1919, however, both firms struck some pennies; those of the Mint, Birmingham, bore a tiny H in the extreme left of the date panel and those struck by the Kings Norton Metal Company had the letters KN in the same place.

Because of their relative scarcity, both H and KN pennies, especially in the higher grades, are generally worth considerably more than the normal issues of the years concerned, as is shown by the following catalogue entries. The examples given are of the more expensive coins.

Pennies

	F	VF	EF
1875 Normal issue	£0·35	£2·00	£7·00
H below date	3·00	15·00	100·00
1912 Normal issue	0·20	1·00	3·00
H in exergue	0·20	2·00	12·50
1918 Normal issue	0·50	1·25	4·00
H in exergue	0·60	6·00	20·00
KN in exergue	0·90	15·00	75·00
1919 Normal issue	0·20	0·60	3·00
H in exergue	0·50	5·00	18·00
KN in exergue	1·25	18·00	85·00

E

Low Tide and Modified Effigy Coins

Two other coin variations which are generally valued well in excess of the normal issues are the so-called Low Tide coins of Edward VII and the Modified Effigy variation of George V.

LOW TIDE COINS

The first issue of pennies of the reign of Edward VII (1901–10) were made in 1902. Though a new die had obviously to be made for the obverse, showing the head of the new king, two distinct dies were used for the reverse. The first die was a new one on which the horizon of the sea on the right of the coin meets the lower legs of Britannia almost exactly at the point where they cross.

The second reverse, however, was struck from dies used for the Victoria penny, dated 1901, in which the horizon meets the lower legs of Britannia *well* below the point at which the left leg disappears behind the right. This coin is the Low Tide variation.

The same variation occurs on both the 1902 halfpennies and farthings; in the case of the farthing the effect upon its value is negligible, but in the case of the halfpenny the price rise is far greater even than that of the penny, as the following catalogue extracts demonstrate.

Penny

	F	VF	EF
1902 Normal sea	£0·20	£1·00	£2·25
Low tide variation	1·00	7·00	20·00

Halfpenny

	F	VF	EF
1902 Normal sea	£0·20	£0·80	£2·50
Low tide variation	5·00	15·00	50·00

MODIFIED EFFIGY COINS

If you study the bronze coins of Edward VII and the issues of George V up to 1926, you will find on many of the reverses a faint outline or 'ghost' of the head on the obverse side.

The reason for this ghosting is a highly technical matter involving such things as metal stress and the appropriateness of the design for the particular metal composition, and well beyond the scope of this book.

'In 1925,' writes C. N. Peck, 'Sir Bertram Mackennal undertook to try to eliminate this "ghosting" on the bronze (and silver) coinage, and to this end he produced a new obverse with the so-called "modified effigy". This was used for the halfpennies dated 1925 and for the pennies and farthings of the following year but, although it was an improvement, it did not entirely correct the defect and it was not until the small head was introduced in 1928 that "ghosting" was still further reduced to what may well be the minimum attainable with these two designs.'

In the modified effigy the head of the king is slightly smaller than hitherto, and the hair, beard and moustache have been retouched. From an identification point of view, however, the important thing is the position of the designer's initials, B.M. (Bertram Mackennal). Up to and including some coins issued in 1926 the initials are relatively large, are just right of centre on the truncation and have a stop after each letter.

On the modified-effigy silver coins (all, that is, except the florin) the head details are identical with those on the bronze coinage, and in addition the beading on the reverse is more pronounced than previously.

Some of the modified-effigy coins are very much more valuable than their unmodified counterparts, as can be seen in the catalogue extracts below:

Penny

	F	VF	EF
1926 First issue of this year	£0·30	£2·50	£10·00
Modified effigy	2·25	25·00	85·00

Halfcrown

	F	VF	EF
1926 First issue of this year	£1·00	£7·00	£37·50
Modified effigy	3·50	13·00	65·00

The above figures also emphasize once again the importance of a coin's condition; a VF 1926 modified effigy penny is more than ten times the price of one which is only Fine and the EF coin is between three and a half and four times as valuable as the VF coin. In the case of the halfcrown an improvement of one grade quadruples its catalogue value.

CHAPTER TWENTY-TWO

Forgeries

The traditional picture of forgers at work is of somewhat rough, uncouth characters working in cobwebbed cellars, pouring base metal into moulds, laboriously making florins or half-crowns, to be used sooner or later by confederates to make small purchases in local greengrocers' or tobacconists' shops.

Today nothing could be further from the truth. The modern coin forger is more likely to be a highly skilled chemist, metallurgist or electronic engineer, or a consortium of all three, perhaps working under the guidance of a highly experienced numismatist. Also, the coins they would produce would not be low-value current issues but almost foolproof copies of high-value gold coins or scarce pieces from Ancient Greek times to the present day.

Furthermore, these coins would be of the correct metal composition and weight. A forged gold two-pound piece would be identical in weight and in gold content to the genuine coin. Clearly the expense of producing one is justified by the price that the genuine article commands in the numismatic market.

For instance, a halfcrown of Edward VII dated 1905 has a silver bullion value of perhaps 30p (it is 92·5% silver); if, just before decimalization did away with the denomination, you had been foolish enough to tender it for some purchase in a shop it would have been worth exactly two shillings and sixpence (12½p), but numismatically it is catalogued as follows: F: £20; VF: £76; EF: £240.

Incidentally, there *are* a number of forgeries of this coin in existence, so *every* 1905 halfcrown should be regarded with suspicion and treated as a possible forgery unless it has been authenticated by the Royal Mint or vouched for by a reputable coin dealer or coin auctioneer.

In recent years there have also been a large number of forged Victorian Old Head gold two-pound pieces in circulation, which have been offered to collectors in Uncirculated condition for £30–£40 instead of their catalogue price of at least £70.

It is wise, therefore, not to buy 'bargains' from people you don't know very well or from advertisements in the personal columns of magazines or newspapers, but to stick to reputable dealers or coin auctions run by firms well known in the numismatic world.

There are also large numbers of forged sovereigns in existence; the reason for this is most interesting.

Shortly after the World War II a large number of 'sovereigns' were minted on the Continent, particularly in Switzerland, where these were sold quite openly. The coins, of correct gold content and excellently engraved and produced, were sold at numismatic values.

The British Government protested, implying that the firms concerned were guilty of forgery. The latter denied this, arguing that the sovereign was no longer produced, nor was it in general circulation in Britain and, therefore, technically they were committing no monetary offence.

To counter this the British Government started in 1958 to mint sovereigns again; these were struck every year up to 1967 except for 1961–62, and can be purchased by any collector.

It is, of course, not only modern coins which have been forged. Large numbers of excellent copies of ancient Roman and Greek coins have issued from the ateliers of dishonest craftsmen over the ages and have been sold not only to tourists visiting sites of excavations such as Pompeii, but to experienced collectors who have accepted them as genuine.

Two or three years ago, as an advertising 'gimmick', a firm of chemists produced copies of some classical coins which, though they would not deceive any experienced collector (nor were they intended so to do), could easily be passed off and sold as genuine coins by some unscrupulous person to an inexperienced collector.

So far I have dealt only with forgeries of complete coins. It is not always necessary to forge the whole of a coin however, it may be enough to alter part of a common genuine coin to make it resemble one of, say, some rare date.

A short time ago, for instance, a friend of mine, a well-known numismatist in the West of England, showed me a 1954 penny. According to official records, no pennies bearing this date were issued for circulation, but a small number were made for die-testing purposes, and all of them, along with the reserve die, were afterwards destroyed. One example escaped destruction, however, as it was found in circulation. The history of this one recorded specimen which 'got away' is well known, and at the time of writing is in America and priced at several thousand pounds, which makes it the most valuable penny in the world. Yet here was another, apparently genuine 1954 penny; had another one 'got away'?

Obviously one suspected a forgery, for I have seen a number of 1933 pennies (another extremely rare coin) which have all turned out to be clever forgeries, but it wasn't until I inspected it under a powerful light with an X20 magnifying glass that I found out how it had been made.

Someone had obviously taken a 1953 penny, bored out the figure 3 and inserted a figure 4 cut out from some other copper coin. It was a brilliant example of precision workmanship and only the faintest hair crack was visible where the plug had been inserted.

One sometimes wonders at the motives which inspire the manufacture of coins of this nature. A master craftsman must realize that such a rarity is bound to be subject to the very closest scrutiny by men who have spent a lifetime vetting such objects. The alteration to the final figure, no matter how well executed, will inevitably be discovered under microscopic examination.

Furthermore such coins are rarely if ever brought to public

notice by their creators, and, perhaps even more strange, they almost always seem to be found by someone in their change.

My guess is that the craftsman concerned is trying to fool the experts, but without the risk of any possible adverse publicity to himself or of prosecution for forgery should the work be ascribed to him. No doubt he scans the papers to see if his 'masterpiece' makes the headlines in either the national or the numismatic press, and is delighted if some rash 'expert' pronounces the coin to be genuine.

How Does One Detect a Forgery?

I must make it quite clear that there are no hard and fast methods which will guarantee the discovery of a forged coin. Obviously there are degrees of expertise in forgery, and master forgers can fool many experts at least some of the time.

Poorly executed forgeries can be discovered by most collectors. Inspection through a powerful magnifying glass will soon discover obvious cracks, hair-lines or crudely executed engraving or striking. In the case of expertly produced coins, however, discovery is largely a matter of experience, allied with an instinct or sixth-sense that something is 'not quite right' either with the appearance or the 'feel' of the coin. Weight is another good guide, for coins are made to very fine tolerances of weight.

However one must ultimately come back to the most important rule of all: rare or valuable coins offered from any but the unimpeachable sources of old-established dealers and firms of the highest integrity must always be suspect until proved otherwise.

Today one has some protection from the provisions of the Trades Descriptions Act, which make it an offence to give a false or misleading description of an article put up for sale, but this cannot prevent a dubious dealer (or forger) selling a coin to a collector and then disappearing before the coin is proved not to be genuine, or a straight dealer innocently offering a forgery in the belief that it is genuine.

CHAPTER TWENTY-THREE

Foreign Coins

How does one set about making a collection of foreign coins?

First bear in mind the principle set out earlier in this book that if you try to buy everything, you end up with nothing. It is much better to specialize, say, in the coins of one country or in something like official proof-sets of a limited number of countries so that you acquire a collection of coins in the best possible condition. In the long run the first of these courses is far better, for over a period of time one will begin to acquire a wide knowledge of the coinage of the country of your choice.

Incidentally, if you live within reasonable reach of London you can always go to the Department of Coins and Medals at the British Museum and study the coins in which you are particularly interested, thus gaining invaluable knowledge for your future collection.

One of the first essentials, however, is to acquire an up-to-date catalogue or reference book of the coins of your selected country. Such books can usually be obtained through any well-known coin dealer, who will be pleased to advise you as to suitable texts. As the number of numismatic books is extremely large any specialized list will soon be out of date, so I have given below merely a list of helpful books.

WORLD COINS

Coins, Ancient Mediaeval and Modern, R. A. G. Carson
Gold Coins of the World, R. Friedberg
Crowns of the World, G. Galletta
A Catalogue of the World's Most Popular Coins, F. Reinfeld
Current Coins of the World, R. S. Yeoman
Coins of the World 1750–1850, W. D. Craig

A Catalogue of Modern World Coins, R. S. Yeoman
Coins in History, J. Porteous
The Coins of the British Commonwealth of Nations to the End of the Reign of George VI, F. Pridmore
The Guidebook and Catalogue of British Commonwealth Coins, J. Renwick, H. Linecar and S. James
The Crown Pieces of Great Britain and the British Commonwealth, H. W. A. Linecar
Coins of the British World from AD 500 to the Present, R. Friedburg
A Guidebook of Modern European Coins, R. P. Harris
A Guidebook of Modern Latin Coins, R. P. Harris
Copper Coins of Europe till 1892, F. C. Higgins
The Dollars of Africa, Asia and Oceania, J. S. Davenport
A Catalogue of the Coins of British Oceania, R. L. Clarke
The Coins of India, C. J. Brown
An Encyclopaedia of Chinese Coins, A. B. Coole
Eight Reales and Pesos of the New World, C. Elizondo
Silver Crowns of the Far East, M. Oka
A Guidebook of Modern United States Currency, N. Shafer
Modern Copper Coins of the Muhammadan States, W. H. Valentine
Central American Coinage Since 1821, H. Wallace
A Guidebook of United States Coins, R. S. Yeoman
Standard Catalogue of British Coins, P. J. Seaby

Having made a general study of the coins in which you are interested, I suggest that you then go to a reputable numismatic firm, tell them of your interest and ask their advice. You must also make quite clear your financial limitations, for they will then be able to guide you along your best economic path. You must always remember that though such dealers make a living from selling coins they are also interested in them, and they are also aware that the wiser their advice to you the longer you are going to buy from them and advise other collectors to do likewise.

As a way of starting your collection, the following twenty suggestions might be considered.

1. A Dollar Type-set of the United States of America

2. A Type-set of the coins of Canada
3. A Type-set of the coins of the West Indies
4. Coins of the South Sea Islands
5. A 20th Century Type-set of the coins of Japan
6. Coins of the Central American States
7. Coins of Australia and/or New Zealand
8. Coins of British India
9. Coins of Central Africa
10. Coins of Scandinavia
11. Modern Russian coins
12. Coins of Spain and/or Portugal
13. Coins of Middle-Eastern countries
14. Coins of Individual European countries
15. Coins of the French Revolution
16. Coins of the Balkan countries
17. Coins of South America or individual South American States
18. Coins of Greece and the Ionian Islands
19. Crown-size coins of Europe since 1900
20. Crown-size coins of the New World

You should always ensure, however, that your coins are genuine, and produced under government authorization. If such is not the case, serious numismatists will doubt a coin's genuineness. In *Current World Coins* R. S. Yeoman provides the following list of coins at present held to be controversial, some of them on the grounds that they were not issued as current coinage but more as collectors' pieces.

Albania	1968 (silver) 5, 10, 25 leke (gold), 20, 50, 100, 200 leke
Andorra	1960, 1963–65 (silver) 25 and 50 dinars
Anguilla	'Liberty Dollar' counterstamped on seven crown-size coins of Mexico, Panama, Peru, Philippines and the Yemen
Bahamas	1967 (gold) 10, 20, 50 and 100 dollars

Bhutan	1966 3 rupees (silver). 1, 2 and 5 sertums (gold) and 1, 2 and 5 sertums (platinum)
Botswana	1966 50 cents (silver) and 10 thebes (gold)
Burundi	1962 and 1965. Gold 10, 25, 50 and 100 francs. 1966 (silver) 100 and 500 francs, Mwambutsa IV 1966 silver 10, 25, 50, 100,500 francs, Ntare V
Chile	1968 5 and 10 pesos (silver) and 50, 100, 200 and 500 pesos (gold)
Colombia	1968 Gold 100, 200, 300, 500 and 1,500 pesos
Congo	1965 Gold 10, 20, 25, 50 and 100 francs
Cuba	1965 Silver souvenir peso
Ethiopia	1966 Gold 10, 20, 50, 100 and 200 dollars
Gabon	1960 Gold 10, 25, 50 and 100 francs
Haiti	1967 Silver 5, 10 and 25 gourdes and gold 20, 50, 100, 200 and 1,000 gourdes
	1968 Silver as for 1967. Gold as for 1967
Hungary	1968 Silver 50 and 100 forints. Gold 50, 100, 200, 500 and 1,000 forints
Ivory Coast	1966 Silver 10 francs and gold 10, 25, 50 and 100 francs
Kenya	1966 Gold 100, 250 and 500 shillings
Isle of Man	1965 Gold, £5, sovereign and half-sovereign
Lesotho	1966 Silver 5, 10, 20 and 50 licente. Gold 1, 2 and 4 maloti
Liberia	1964 Gold 20 dollars
	1965 12, 25 and 30 dollars
Liechenstein	1961 Gold 25 and 50 franken
Lundy Island	1965
Mali	1960 Silver 10 francs
	1967 Gold 10, 25, 50 and 100 francs
Monaco	1966 10 francs Marriage Coin. Gold, 200 francs
Nicaragua	1967 Gold 50 cordobas
Niger	1960 Silver 500 and 1,000 francs. Gold 10, 25, 50 and 100 francs
	1968 Silver 10 francs. Gold, as for 1960

Paraguay	1968 Gold 10,000 guaranies
Rhodesia	1966 Gold 10 shillings and 1 and 5 pounds
Rwandi	1961 Gold 10, 25, 50 and 100 francs
Senegal	1968 Gold 10, 25, 50 and 100 francs
Sharjah	1964 Silver 5 rupees (Kennedy)
Somalia	1965 Gold 20, 50, 100, 200 and 500 scellini
Swaziland	1968 Silver 5, 10, 20, 50 cents and 1 luhlangi and Gold 1 lilangeni
Thailand	1968 Gold 150, 300 and 600 baht
Tonga	1962 Gold $\frac{1}{4}$, $\frac{1}{2}$ and 1 koula
	1967 Palladium $\frac{1}{4}$, $\frac{1}{2}$ and 1 hau
	1968 As above but with 1968 counterstamp
Tunisia	1967 Gold 2, 5, 10, 24 and 40 dinars
Yemen (Royalist)	1965 Silver 'Churchill' 1 rial

It is interesting to note that in the 37 countries listed above no less than 27 of them issued gold coins (which of course could be sold at a higher value as coins than as bullion), and that of these, nine issued the coins in 1965 and 1966.

The fact that there is some controversy about the above issues does not mean, of course, that you should not buy them. Many of them are beautiful 'coins' and well worth collecting, if only as works of art, and in time, no doubt they could increase in value.

CHAPTER TWENTY-FOUR

Non-coins

Over the last four years a large number of readers of my *Daily Telegraph* column *Collecting Coins* have written to me about or sent for my identification the following 'coins':

1. A sovereign-sized, gold-coloured 'coin' with the head of George III on the obverse and a shield-like design on the reverse, looking very much like a 'spade guinea'.
2. Another gold-coloured sovereign-sized 'coin' with the young head of Queen Victoria on the obverse and a design looking somewhat like St George and the Dragon on the reverse.
3. A wide variety of copper and bronze 'coins' bearing inscriptions such as 'Model Farthing' and 'Model Sovereign'.
4. A silver, shilling-sized 'coin' with the young head of Victoria on one side and the old head of the Queen on the other side.

None of these is a coin of the realm; the first two are virtually valueless, the third worth only a few shillings and of little interest to numismatists except the small number who collect numismatic and pseudo-numismatic curiosities; the fourth is a commemorative medallion.

The Imitation Spade Guinea

Many new collectors and members of the general public have been deceived by the imitation spade guineas and have bought them as genuine gold coins.

I cannot do better than quote the pamphlet on the subject issued by the British Museum Department of Coins and Medals:

'One of the commonest objects sent up for identification to this Department is a playing-card counter made in imitation of the guineas and half-guineas of George III, issued between 1787 and 1800, nicknamed "spade guineas" from the shape of the shield on the reverse. These counters are made of brass – sometimes so burnished as to lead people to take them for gold. They are extremely common, in fact brand new specimens have been known to be offered for sale till quite recently at 100 for 2/6 [12½p]. The legends should read: GEORGIUS III DEI GRATIA, and on the back M(agniae) B(ritanniae) F(ranciae) ET H(iberniae) REX F(idei) D(efensor) B(runswicensis) ET L(uneburgensis) D(ux) S(acri) R(omani) I(mperii) A(rchi-) T(hesaurarius) ET E(lector); that is, George III by the Grace of God King of Great Britain, France & Ireland, Defender of the Faith, Duke of Brunswick and Luneburg, High Treasurer & Elector of the Holy Roman Empire. They are, however, usually bungled, with the date altered. Sometimes they bear the words: IN MEMORY OF THE GOOD OLD DAYS, or also the name of some business firm, or the word B.I.R.M. for Birmingham.'

Hanover 'Jacks'

When Victoria came to the throne in 1837 she was unable also to succeed to that of Hanover because of the Salic Law which forbade the succession of women.

Therefore her uncle, the Duke of Cumberland, became the ruler of that country and left England for that purpose. Though he seems to have been administratively capable, he was not popular with the British Establishment, whose members were pleased to see him go.

As was the custom at the time, commemorative medals or medalets were struck on the slightest provocation and this occasion was no exception, for brass, sovereign-sized satirical medalets, which were virtually 'good-riddance' propaganda items, were produced in great numbers.

On the obverse is a representation (not very well done) of the young head of Queen Victoria, with the legend VICTORIA REGINA and on the reverse a design, which on a casual glance, looks somewhat similar to the Pistrucci St George and the Dragon, in that a figure on horseback is trampling on a three-headed, dragon-like creature. Above the figure is the legend TO HANOVER, while below is the date 1837 in the exergue.

It is of interest to note that some forty years or so after their original issue a large number of these medalets reappeared with a variety of dates on the obverse instead of the reverse, this time, it is believed, with some criminal intent, for the medalets could quite easily be mistaken for sovereigns if passed in crowded places. The producers of these medalets could not be accused of forgery, however, since no genuine Victoria sovereigns were ever produced with the date on the obverse and the St George and the Dragon design on the reverse.

As has already been stated, these medalets are virtually worthless, though they are of some historical interest as an example of Victorian methods of political propaganda.

Model Coins

In the late Victoria and Edwardian period large numbers of tiny, often beautifully executed, 'model' coins were produced commercially (a large number came from Germany) for use in children's games and Christmas crackers or as card counters. Most of them have legends such as 'Model Penny', 'Model Halfpenny', 'Coronation Model Sovereign' (King Edward VII's head) and so on. Some of them were issued as boxed sets consisting of a model sovereign, penny, halfpenny and farthing; such sets are sought after by collectors of numismatic curiosities and as beautiful examples of the coin engraver's art.

A quite different type of model coin, usually larger than those above and with a circular, silver-coloured central inset were also issued by a Birmingham medallist as serious suggestions for a new-design currency. These too are sought after by some collectors, even though they are not genuine coins.

Diamond Jubilee Medalets

In 1897, to commemorate the sixtieth year of Queen Victoria's reign some shilling-sized and larger commemorative medals were officially produced and sold publicly. On one side is the Young Head of the Queen as she was on her accession and on the other the well-known veiled Old Head.

The smaller coins are often erroneously thought to be shillings (their selling price at the time of issue actually was one shilling). As medals they are sought after, and in VF or better condition can be bought for about £1.

Another common medalet, often thought to be a penny (as it is almost exactly the same size) and dated 1897 shows four generations of the Royal Family – Queen Victoria and the future Edward VII, George V and Edward VIII – all surmounted by a crown radiate. On the reverse are three shields bearing the Irish harp, the rampant lion of Scotland and the three leopards of England, surmounted by a crown. The legend quite clearly states THE DIAMOND JUBILEE. TO COMMEMORATE THE 60TH YEAR OF HER MAJESTY'S REIGN. 1837–1897. Incidentally, a useful tip to remember when trying to tell whether a coin is a genuine British issue is to remember that from the time of the Commonwealth, when Cromwell's head was used, no coin has borne the head(s) of other than the actual ruler(s) of the country, with the single exception of the 1965 Churchill crown.

F

CHAPTER TWENTY-FIVE

In Conclusion: Some Current Trends

Two types of numismatic objects that have recently started to attract a great deal of interest are British tokens and banknotes. From an investment viewpoint, therefore, now is the time to start making a collection of these two items.

Tokens

At various times in our history, and particularly at the end of the seventeenth century, the end of the eighteenth and beginning of the nineteenth, the British Government, either because of incompetence or through indifference to the needs of the public in general and especially those of the trade, failed to issue the coins of small denomination vital to the conduct of normal day-to-day business. To overcome these difficulties, business firms, shopkeepers and even inns and taverns began to issue their own tokens in both copper and silver. At first the use of any individual token would be limited to the buying of goods at the business place of the issuer or in the immediate locality, but gradually their use would be extended and many of them would become freely interchangeable.

Some of the early issues were relatively crude, but many, particularly those struck from 1787 onwards (starting with pennies and halfpennies struck by the Anglesey Copper Mining Company) were truly works of art.

As with coins, the values of tokens are closely related to their condition; well-circulated and obviously worn specimens, unless extremely rare, are of little interest either to dealers or to collectors.

The following books will be found helpful:

The Provincial Token Coinage of the Eighteenth Century, Dalton and Hamer

The Nineteenth Century Token Coinage of Great Britain, Ireland, The Channel Islands and the Isle of Man, W. J. Davis
Trade Tokens Issued in the Seventeenth Century, G. C. Williamson
The Silver Token-Coinage mainly issued between 1811–12, R. Dalton
Commercial Coins 1787–1804, R. C. Bell
Copper Commercial Coins 1811–1819, R. C. Bell

An invaluable book for your own library is Seaby's catalogue *British Tokens and their Values*, edited by Peter Seaby and Monica Bussell.

Banknotes

For many years only a relatively small number of numismatists have collected banknotes, but recently there has been an extremely sharp rise in interest. In the United Kingdom this is almost certainly due to decimalization and the disappearance of the ten-shilling note. As a consequence the values of Extremely Fine or Uncirculated notes have risen considerably, as have those of the early notes issued during the First World War.

Banknotes are graded in a similar manner to coins; the six grades normally used are:

MINT. A note which has never been in circulation, is flat and not creased in any way whatsoever.

EXTREMELY FINE. Shows no signs of having been in circulation; it is still crisp but may have been folded.

VERY FINE. Shows slight signs of circulation and of having been folded; the edges may have slight signs of wear and there may be pinholes but the note is still clean and has not been torn in any way.

FINE. The note has obviously been folded and creased several times; it may bear bank cashiers' ink markings and has small tears around the edges.

FAIR. Has obviously been in circulation for a long time. It is dirty; the edges are frayed and have small tears in places; it may have been written on but nevertheless the note is still intact. As with coins, notes in this condition are of little or no interest either to collectors or dealers unless they are rare issues.

POOR. A note which can still be identified but is not fully legible, and parts may be missing. Unless of great rarity a note in this condition is not considered worth collecting at all.

The axiom that if you collect everything you end up by collecting nothing applies no less to banknotes. New collectors are advised to specialize in, say, the notes of one country, or military notes issued during wartime, or even the notes designed by a specific engraver or issued by a particular company.

Collecting notes can be as expensive or as inexpensive as your financial means will permit. Some notes, such as those issued in Germany during the post-World-War I inflationary period, or American Confederate Currency, can be purchased at a very low cost; on the other hand some early United Kingdom notes can be quite expensive.

All collectors of banknotes (and particularly those who are just starting a collection) are strongly advised to become members of the International Bank Note Society. The subscription is £2·50 p.a., and full details of membership can be obtained from Mr F. Philipson, 5 Windermere Road, Beeston, Nottingham, NG9 3AS, or from the Secretary/Treasurer, Mrs A. B. Hill, Jnr, 4944 Lindell Boulevard, St Louis, Missouri, 63108, USA.

Among the advantages of membership are:

A Quarterly Journal published in March, June, September and December containing articles by experts on banknotes and their collection.

Postal Auctions for members only, usually run twice a year.

Membership Directory. Each year a Directory is published which lists all members plus their collecting interests enabling collectors with similar interests to make contact with each other should they so wish.

Note Identification. The Society has an expert committee for note identification of which any member can avail himself of its services by sending a photostat copy of the obverse and reverse of the note(s) he wishes to be identified.

Library. A library of books and slides is kept in the United States; these can be borrowed by members for the cost of both-ways postage.

A Technical and Research Consultant. This post was established for the purpose of aiding all those interested in academic research in the many facets of the collecting of paper money.

Books for Information

The following books will be of interest and value to those interested in collecting banknotes:

Collecting Paper Money, Colin Narbeth

North American Currency, The Standard Paper Money Reference, Grover C. Criswell, Jnr

World War II Allied Military Currency, R. S. Toy

World War II Axis Military Currency, R. S. Toy and B. Meyer

Catalogue of United States, Canadian and Confederate Currency, R. Werlich

Bank of England and Treasury Notes, 1694–1970, D. M. Miller

Catalogue of European Paper Money since 1900, Albert Pick

Another interesting new trend is an increasing interest in Chinese coins. This could be well worth watching.

The following books will be found valuable for study and reference:

An Encyclopaedia of Chinese Coins, Vol. 1, A. B. Coole

Coins in China's History, A. B. Coole

Illustrated Catalogue of Chinese Coins, E. Kann

An Illustrated Guide to Chinese Cash Pieces of the Manchu Mints, A. E. H. Petrie

Chinese Currency, F. Schjoth

A Catalogue of Modern World Coins, R. S. Yeoman

Coins of the World, 1750–1850, W. D. Craig

List of Coin Denominations

This list, which is useful for coin identification, includes all denominations of coins used since the middle of the last century, together with the countries that they come from.

Abassi   Afghanistan.
Afghani   Afghanistan.
Agora (*Agorot*)   Israel.
Ahmadi   Yemen.
Amani   Afghanistan.
Amman Cash   Mewar Udaipur, Pudukota (India Native States).
Anna   Burma, India, India Native States, Mombasa, Muscat and Oman, Pakistan.
Argentino   Argentina.
Ashrafi   Bahawalpur, Hyderabad (India Native States).
Att   Thailand (Siam).
Aurar   Iceland.
Avo   Macau (Macao), Timor.

Baht   Thailand (Siam).
Baizah   Muscat and Oman.
Balboa   Panama.
Ban (*Banu, Bani*)   Romania.
Banica   Yugoslavia.
Belga   Belgium.
Besa (*Bese*)   Ethiopia, Italian Somaliland.
Bit   Danish West Indies.
Bogach   Yemen.
Bolivar   Venezuela.
Boliviano   Bolivia.

Cash   China, Chinese Turkestan, Hong Kong, Travancore (India Native State).
Cent   Australia, Bahamas, British Caribbean Territories, British

Honduras, British North Borneo, Canada, Ceylon, China, Curaçao, Danish West Indies, East Africa, East Africa and Uganda, Ethiopia, Guyana, Hawaii, Hong Kong, Kenya, Kiao Chau, Liberia, Malaya, Malaya and British Borneo, Mauritius, Netherlands, Netherlands Antilles, Netherlands East Indies, Newfoundland, New Zealand, Prince Edward Island, Rhodesia, Sarawak, Seychelles, Sierra Leone, Singapore, South Africa, Straits Settlements, Surinam, Trinidad and Tobago, Uganda, United States, Zanzibar.

Centas (*Centu, Centai*) Lithuania.

Centavo Angola, Argentina, Bolivia, Brazil, Cape Verde Islands, Chile, Colombia, Costa Rica, Cuba, Dominican Republic, Ecuador, Guatemala, Honduras, Mexico, Mozambique, Nicaragua, Paraguay, Peru, Philippines, Portugal, Portuguese Guinea, Portuguese India, Puerto Rico, St Thomas and Prince Islands, Salvador, Timor, Venezuela.

Centesimo (*Centesimi*) Chile, Dominican Republic, Italy, Panama, Paraguay, San Marino, Somalia, Uruguay, Vatican City.

Centime Algeria, Belgian Congo, Belgium, Cambodia, Cameroon, Comoro Islands, France, French Cochin China, French Equatorial Africa, French Indo-China, French Oceania, French Polynesia, French Somaliland, French West Africa, Guadeloupe, Guinea, Haiti, Laos, Luxembourg, Madagascar, Martinique, Monaco, Morocco, New Caledonia, Reunion, Switzerland, Togo, Tunisia.

Centimo Costa Rica, Paraguay, Spain, Venezuela.

Chio Formosa (China), Inner Mongolia, Manchukuo.

Chomsihs Tarim and Ghurfah.

Chon Korea, North Korea.

Chuckram Travancore (India Native State).

Colon (*Colones*) Costa Rica, Salvador.

Condor Chile, Colombia, Ecuador.

Cordoba Nicaragua.

Crown Australia, Bermuda, Gibraltar, Great Britain, Ireland, Malawi, New Zealand, Rhodesia and Nyasaland, Southern Rhodesia.

Cruzeiro Brazil.

Dak Nepal.

Daler Danish West Indies.

Decimo   Chile, Colombia, Ecuador.

Decimo De Sucre   Ecuador.

Dime   Hawaii, United States.

Dinar (Dinara)   Algeria, Bahrain, Hejaz, Iraq, Kuwait, Persia, Serbia, Yugoslavia.

Dinero   Peru.

Dirham   Morocco, Qatar and Dubai.

Dokdo (Dokda)   Junagadh, Kutch, Navanager (India Native States).

Dollar   Australia, Bahamas, Canada, China, Fiji, Great Britain, Hawaii, Hong Kong, Jamaica, Liberia, Newfoundland, New Zealand, Singapore, Straits Settlements, United States.

Dong   French Indo-China, North and South Vietnam.

Double   Guernsey.

Drachma (Drachmai)   Crete, Greece.

Dub   Hyderabad (India Native State).

Ducat   Austria, Czechoslovakia, Hungary, Netherlands, Yugoslavia.

Dukat (Dukata)   Yugoslavia.

Eagle (Double, Half and Quarter Eagles)   United States.

Escudo   Angola, Cape Verde Islands, Chile, Mozambique, Portugal, Portuguese Guinea, Portuguese India, St Thomas and Prince Islands, Timor.

Eyrir (Aurar)   Iceland.

Fanam   Travancore (India Native State).

Farthing   Ceylon, Great Britain, Ireland, Jamaica, Malta.

Fen   Manchukuo, Communist China.

Fenig (Fenigow)   Poland.

Filler   Hungary.

Fils   Bahrain, Iran, Jordan, Kuwait, South Arabia.

Florin   Australia, Austria, East Africa, Fiji, Great Britain, Hungary, Ireland, Malawi, New Zealand, Rhodesia and Nyasaland, South Africa.

Forint   Hungary.

Franc   Algeria, Belgian Congo, Belgium, Burundi, Cambodia, Cameroon, Comoro Islands, Congo (Kinshasa), Danish West Indies, Ecuador, Equatorial Africa, French Indo-China, French Oceania, French Polynesia, French Somaliland, French West

Africa, Guadaloupe, Guinea, Katanga, Luxembourg, Madagascar, Malagasy Republic, Mali, Martinique, Monaco, Morocco, New Caledonia, New Hebrides, Reunion, Ruanda-Urundi, Rwanda, St Pierre and Miquelon, Switzerland, Togo, Tunisia, West African States.

Frang Luxembourg.

Frank (Franken) Belgium, Liechtenstein, Saarland, Switzerland.

Franka Albania.

Franka ari Albania.

Fuang Thailand (Siam).

Fun Korea.

Gersh Ethiopia.

Girsh Nejd, Hejaz, Saudi Arabia.

Golde Sierra Leone.

Goumier Morocco.

Gourde Haiti.

Groat Great Britain.

Groschen Austria, Germany (States).

Grosz (Grosze, Groszy) Poland.

Guerche Egypt.

Guinea Saudi Arabia, Great Britain.

Gulden Curaçao, Danzig, Netherlands, Netherlands Antilles, Netherlands East Indies, Surinam.

Halala Saudi Arabia, Yemen.

Haler (Halierov, Halere, Haleru) Bohemia and Moravia, Czechoslovakia.

Half-Dime United States.

Hao French Indo-China, North Vietnam.

Heller Austria, German East Africa.

Hwan South Korea.

Imadi Yemen.

Kapang Sarawak.

Kopec Poland.

Kopek (Kopeck) Russia, Tuva.

Kori Kutch (India Native State).

Korona Hungary.

Koruna (Koruny, Korun)   Bohemia and Moravia, Czechoslovakia, Slovakia.
Krajczar (Kreuzer)   Hungary.
Kran   Persia.
Kreuzer   Austria, Hungary.
Krona (Kroner)   Sweden.
Krona (Kronur)   Iceland.
Krone (Kronen)   Austria–Hungary, Leichtenstein.
Krone (Kroner)   Denmark, Greenland, Norway.
Kroon (Krooni)   Estonia.
Kuna (Kune)   Yugoslavia, Croatia.
Kurus   Turkey.
Kyat   Burma.

Larin (Lari)   Maldive Islands.
Lats (Lati)   Latvia.
Lek (Leku, Leke)   Albania.
Lempira   Honduras.
Leone   Sierra Leone.
Lepton (Lepta)   Crete, Greece.
Lev (Leva)   Bulgaria.
Li   Manchukuo.
Libra   Peru.
Likuta (Makuta)   Congo (Kinshasa).
Lira (Lire)   Eritrea, Italian Somaliland, Israel, Italy, San Marino, Syria, Turkey, Vatican City.
Litas (Litu, Litai)   Lithuania.

Mace   China, Chinese Turkestan.
Macuta   Angola.
Makuta   Congo (Kinshasa).
Maravedis (Maravedi)   Spain.
Mark   Estonia, Germany, German New Guinea.
Markka (Markkaa)   Finland.
Matona   Ethiopia.
Mazuna   Morocco.
Mil   Cyprus, Hong Kong, Israel, Palestine.
Millième   Tunisia.
Milreis (1,000 Reis)   Brazil, Portugal.
Miscals   Chinese Turkestan.

Mohar Nepal.
Mohur India, Bikanir, Cooch Behar, Gwalior, Hyderabad, Rajkot (India Native States).
Mongo Mongolia.
Mun Korea.

Naya Paisa (Naye Paise) Bhutan, India.
Ngwee Zambia.

Onza Costa Rica.
Ore Denmark, Faroe Islands, Greenland, Norway.
Öre Sweden.

Pa'anga Tonga.
Pahlevi Persia.
Pai Hyderabad (India Native State).
Paisa (Paise) Bahawalpur, Bhutan, Ratlam (India Native States), Nepal, Pakistan.
Paissa Afghanistan.
Para Hejaz, Montenegro, Serbia, Turkey, Yugoslavia.
Pardao Portuguese India.
Pataca Macau (Macao), Timor.
Pengo Hungary.
Penni (Pennia) Finland.
Penny (Pence) Australia, British Guiana, British West Africa, Ceylon, Fiji, The Gambia, Ghana, Great Britain, Guernsey, Ireland, Jamaica, Malawi, Mauritius, New Guinea, New Zealand, Nigeria, Rhodesia, Rhodesia and Nyasaland, South Africa, Southern Rhodesia, Zambia.
Perper (Perpera) Montenegro.
Pesa German East Africa.
Peseta Peru, Spain, Viscayan Republic.
Presewa Ghana.
Peso Argentina, Chile, Colombia, Costa Rica, Cuba, Dominican Republic, Guatemala, Honduras, Mexico, Paraguay, Philippines, Puerto Rico, Salvador, Uruguay.
Pfennig Danzig, German New Guinea, Germany.
Piastre Cyprus, Egypt, French Cochin China, French Indo-China, Lebanon, Libya, Sudan, Syria, Tonkin, Tunisia, Turkey, United Arab Republic.

Pice   Bhutan, East Africa, India, Mombasa, Pakistan.
Pie   India, Pakistan.
Pond   South African Republic.
Pound   Egypt, Great Britain, Israel, Rhodesia, South Africa, Syria, Turkey, United Arab Republic.
Pruta   Israel.
Puffin   Lundy.
Pul   Afghanistan.
Pya   Burma.
Pysa   Zanzibar.

Qindar Ari   Albania.
Qindarka   Albania.
Qindar Leku   Albania.
Qiran   Afghanistan.
Quarter   United States.
Quartillo   Spain.
Quarto   Philippines, Spain.
Quetzal   Guatemala.

Rand   South Africa.
Reaal   Curaçao.
Real (Reales)   Chile, Colombia, Costa Rica, Dominican Republic, Ecuador, Guatemala, Honduras, Mexico, Peru, Salvador, Spain, Venezuela.
Reichsmark   Germany.
Reichspfennig   Germany.
Reis   Azores, Brazil, Portugal.
Rentenpfennig   Germany (Republic).
Rial   Morocco, Muscat and Oman.
Rigsdaler   Denmark.
Riksdaler   Sweden.
Rin   Japan.
Riyal   Saudi Arabia.
Rouble (or Ruble)   Russia, Soviet Central Asia.
Rupee   Afghanistan, Bhutan, Burma, Ceylon, German East Africa, India, Mauritius, Mombasa, Nepal, Pakistan, Saudi Arabia, Seychelles, Tibet.
Rupia   Italian Somaliland, Portuguese India.
Rupie (Rupien)   German East Africa.

Ryal   Hejaz, Muscat and Oman, Nejd, Persia, Yemen, Zanzibar.

Santims (Santimi)   Latvia.
Sapeque   Annam, French Cochin China, French Indo-China.
Satang   Thailand (Siam).
Schilling   Austria.
Scudo   Bolivia, Chile, Costa Rica, Ecuador, Peru.
Schwaren   Germany (Bremen, Oldenburg).
Sen   Brunei, Cambodia, Indonesia, Japan, Malaysia, West New
Guinea (Irian).
Sene   Western Samoa.
Sengi   Congo (Kinshasa).
Seniti   Tonga.
Senti   Estonia, Tanzania.
Sentimo   Philippines.
Shahi   Afghanistan, Persia.
Shilingi   Tanzania.
Shilling   Australia, British West Africa, Cyprus, East Africa, Fiji,
The Gambia, Ghana, Great Britain, Guernsey, Ireland, Jamaica,
Jersey, Kenya, Malawi, New Guinea, New Zealand, Nigeria,
Rhodesia, Rhodesia and Nyasaland, South Africa, Southern
Rhodesia, Tanzania, Uganda, Zambia.
Sho   Tibet.
Skarung (Skar)   Tibet.
Skilling   Denmark, Norway.
Sol (Soles)   Peru.
Somalo   Somalia.
Sovereign   Australia, Canada, Great Britain, South Africa.
Speciedaler   Norway.
Srang   Tibet.
Stotinka (Stotinki)   Bulgaria.
Stuiver   Curaçao.
Su   French Indo-China, South Vietnam.
Sucre   Ecuador.
Sueldo   Bolivia.

Tala   Western Samoa.
Talari   Eritrea, Ethiopia.
Tanga   Portuguese India.
Tangka   Tibet.

Tenga   Bukhara (Soviet Central Russia State).
Thaler (or Taler)   Austria, Leichtenstein.
Tical   Thailand (Siam).
Toman   Persia.
Trade Dollar   Japan, United States.
Trambiya   Kutch (India Native State).
Tukhrik   Mongolia.

Venezolano   Venezuela.
Vereinsthaler   Austria-Hungary.

Wark   Ethiopia.
Warn   Korea.
Whan   Korea.
Won   Korea, South Korea.

Xu   French Indo-China, North and South Vietnam.

Yang   Korea.
Yen   Japan.
Yuan   China, Communist China.

Zloty (Zlote, Zlotych)   Poland.

Coin Dealers and Auctioneers

There are now coin dealers in most towns and their addresses can usually be found in the trade section of the local telephone directory. Local auctioneers can also be found from the same source.

However there follows a short list of the better-known dealers and auctioneers in the United Kingdom.

Dealers

LONDON

A. H. Baldwin and Sons Ltd. 1–11 John Adam Street, Adelphi, London WC2.

B. A. Seaby Ltd, Audley House, 11 Margaret Street, London W1.

Spink and Son, Ltd, 5 King Street, St James's, London SW1.

L. H. Gance Ltd, 24 Hatton Garden, London EC1.

Eva Hardy, The Coin Cabinet, 15a Grand Buildings, Northumberland Avenue, London WC2.

Maundy Allen, 110 Great Portland Street, London WIN 5PE.

Mayfair Coin Company, 117 Regent Street, London W1.

KENT

Joan E. Allen and Company, 184 Main Road, Biggin Hill, Kent.

LANCASHIRE

Peter Ireland, 13a Clifton Street, Blackpool, Lancs.

R. & L. Coins, 10 Dale Street, Blackpool, Lancs.

Iun Sandiford, 42 Daventry Road, Chorlton, Manchester 21.

MIDDLESEX

Harrow Coin & Stamp Centre, 154 College Road, Harrow, Middx.

NORTHUMBERLAND

Corbitt & Hunter Ltd, 3–5 St Nicholas Buildings, Newcastle-upon-Tyne 1.

STAFFORDSHIRE
Crown Coin Co., 190a Horseley Heath, Tipton.

SUFFOLK
Schwer Coins, Felixstowe Ferry G.C., Felixstowe.

WARWICKSHIRE
Format Coin & Medal Co. Ltd, 269 Broad Street, Birmingham.

WESTMORLAND
Lakeland Coins, 34a Kirkland, Kendal.

WILTSHIRE
F. J. Jeffery & Son Ltd, 18–20 Warwick Crescent, Melksham.

WORCESTERSHIRE
Fellows Coins & Medals, 11 The Tything, Worcester.

YORKSHIRE
Leeds Coin Centre Ltd, PO Box 180, 25 Merrion Street, Leeds 2.

IRISH REPUBLIC (EIRE)
Numismatic Depot, The Jewellery Shop, 19 Merrion Row, Dublin 2.

NORTHERN IRELAND
L. A. Kaitcer (Antiques) Ltd. 89 Dublin Road, Belfast.

SCOTLAND
A. D. Hamilton & Co., 54–6 Bridge Street, Glasgow, C5.

WALES
F. C. Parker, 46–8, Royal Arcade, Cardiff, CF1 2AE.

CHANNEL ISLANDS
Guernsey Stamp & Coin Shop, 15 Mill Street, St Peter Port, Guernsey.

Auctioneers
The following auctioneers normally hold a minimum of six or more coin auctions per year:

Christie, Manson & Woods, 8 King Street, St James's, London SW1.
Forrest and Co., 79/85 Cobbold Road, Leytonstone, London E11.

Glendining & Co. Ltd, Blenstock House, 7 Blenheim Street, London W1.

Great Metropolitan Auction Sales, 115 Lower Clapton Road, London E5.

D. W. Gray, 2 Nottingham Street, London W1.

Sotheby & Co., 34–5 New Bond Street, London W1.

Thimbleby's, Lumley Building, 11 Reading Road, Pangbourne, Berks.

East Anglian Collectors' Auctions, Curtons House, Walpole St Peter, Wisbech, Cambs.

Richard Baker & Baker, 9 Hamilton Street, Birkenhead, Cheshire.

Button, Menhennitt & Mutton Ltd, Belmont Auction Rooms, Wadebridge, Cornwall.

Bearnes & Waycotts, 3 Warren Road, Torquay, Devon.

S. W. Cottee & Son, 10 North Street, Wareham, Dorset.

W. Morey & Sons, 50 East Street, Bridport, Dorset.

H. G. Hughes & Co., Chapel Street, Halstead, Essex.

Spurgeon & Co., 57 Station Road, Clacton-on-Sea, Essex.

A. W. Armour, Picket Croft, Picket Hill, Ringwood, Hants.

Franks & Co. Ltd, 221 Great Western Street, Manchester 14.

S. C. Kirk & Co., 5 Clifton Street, Lytham, Lancs.

A. Lockridge & Co., 25 Horsefair Street, Leicester.

Noel D. Abel, 32 Norwich Road, Watton, Norfolk.

Charles Hawkins & Sons, Bank Chambers, King's Lynn, Norfolk.

Irelands, 13 Castle Meadow, Norwich, Norfolk.

Henry Spencer & Sons, 15 Exchange Street, Retford, Notts.

Laver and Son, 17 High Street, Glastonbury, Somerset.

West Coin Auctions, 88 Benedict Street, Glastonbury, Somerset.

E. Reeves Ltd, 110–120 Church Street, Croydon, Surrey.

King & Chasemore, Station Road, Pulborough, Sussex.

Michaels & Michaels, Norton Lea, Upper Norton, Selsey, Sussex.

Wallis & Wallis, All Saints House, 210 High Street, Lewes, Sussex.

Cecil Cariss & Son, 20–2 High Street, King's Heath, Birmingham.

Fellows & Parkes, 11 The Tything, Worcester.

E. J. Whitt & Ridley, 8 Pierpoint Street, Worcester.

John W. Ackroyd & Son, 31 Sunbridge Road, Bradford 1.

Bibliography

General

R. A. G. Carson, *Coins – Ancient, Medieval and Modern*, 642 p. Hutchinson, 1962.

W. D. Craig, *Coins of the World, 1750–1850*, 753 p. Whitman Pub. Co., 1966.

P. Finn and A. Dowle, *Coins for Pleasure and Investment*, 182 p. Gifford, 1970.

R. Friedberg, *Gold Coins of the World from AD 600*, 384 p. Oak Tree Press, 1970.

H. Linecar, *An Advanced Guide to Coin Collecting*, 287 p. Pelham Books, 1970.

C. Narbeth, *Coins and Currency*, 127 p. Muller, 1966.

F. Purvey, *Collecting Coins*, 96 p. Foyle, 1964.

J. Porteous, *Coins in History* 256 p. Weidenfeld & Nicolson, 1969.

G. B. Rawlins, *Coins and How to Know Them: Ancient, Medieval and Modern*, 366 p. 1966.

R. S. Yeoman, *Current Coins of the World*, 264 p. Western Pub. Co., 1971.

R. S. Yeoman, *A Catalogue of Modern World Coins, 1850–1964*, 509 p. Whitman Pub. Co., 1959.

G. Galleta, *Crowns of the World*, Oak Tree Press, 1965.

F. Reinfeld, *A Catalogue of the Coin's Most Popular Coins*, 416 p. Oak Tree Press, 1959.

H. W. A. Linecar, *Beginner's Guide to Coin Collecting*, Pelham, 1966.

M. Amstell, *A Start to Coin Collecting*, Foulsham, 1966.

Greek Coins

B. V. Head, *A Guide to the Principal Coins of the Greeks*, 108 p. British Museum, 1959.

C. M. Kraay and M. Hirmer, *Greek Coins*, 396 p. Thames & Hudson, 1966.

Z. H. Klawans, *An Outline of Ancient Greek Coins*, 208 p. Oak Tree Press, 1970.

Roman Coins

G. Askew, *The Coinage of Roman Britain*, 88 p. Seaby, 1968.

H. A. Grueber, *Coins of the Roman Republic in the British Museum*, 3 vols, 1,432 p. rev. ed. British Museum, 1970.

D. R. Sear, *Roman Coins and Their Values*, 376 p. Seaby, 1964.

British Coins

J. J. Cullimore Allen, *Sovereigns of the British Empire*, 60 p. Spink, 1965.

R. C. Bell, *Commercial Coins, 1787–1804*, 320 p. Corbitt & Hunter, 1964.

G. C. Brooke, *English Coins*, 300 p. Methuen, 1966.

R. Dalton, *The Silver Token Coinage, 1811–12*, 63 p. Waters, 1968.

R. Dalton and H. S. Hamer, *The Provincial Token Coinage of the 18th Century*, 3 vols, 567 p. repr. Seaby, 1967.

J. Edmundson, *Collecting Modern British Coins*, 216 p. Pelham, 1970.

P. Finn and A. Dowle, *The Guide Book to the Coinage of Ireland*, 128 p. Spink, 1969.

H. A. Grueber, *Handbook of Coins of Great Britain and Ireland in the British Museum*, repr. Seaby, 1971.

H. A. Grueber and C. F. Keary, *Anglo-Saxon Coins in the British Museum*, 2 vols. 822 p. repr. Seaby, 1970.

R. L. Kenyon, *Gold Coins of England*, 237 p. repr. Firecrest Pub. Co., 1970.

H. W. A. Linecar and A. G. Stone, *English Proof and Pattern Crown-Size Pieces, 1658–1960*, 116 p. Spink, 1968.

J. North, *English Hammered Coinage, Vol. I, c. 650–1272*, 200 p. Spink, 1964.

J. North, *English Hammered Coinage, Vol. II, 1272–1662*, 183 p. Spink, 1961.

C. W. Peck, *English Copper, Tin and Bronze Coins in the British Museum, 1558–1958*, 651 p. 2nd ed., British Museum, 1964.

P. J. Seaby, *Standard Catalogue of British Coins*, 280 p. Seaby, 1970.

P. J. Seaby and M. Bussell, *British Copper Coins and Their Values*, 96 p. Seaby, 1970.

H. A. Seaby and P. A. Rayner, *The English Silver Coinage from 1649*, 203 p. Seaby, 1968.

I. Stewart, *The Scottish Coinage*, 215 p. Spink, 1955.

K. E. Bressett, *A Guidebook of English Coins, 19th and 20th Centuries*,

128 p. 7th ed., Whitman Pub. Co., 1969.

H. W. A. Linecar, *The Crown Pieces of Great Britain, 1658–1960*, 102 p. rev. ed. Benn, 1969.

P. Seaby, *Coins and Tokens of Ireland*, 167 p. Seaby, 1970.

W. J. Davis, *The 19th Century Token Coinage of Great Britain, Ireland, etc.*, 284 p. repr. Seaby, 1969.

G. C. Williamson, *Trade Tokens issued in the 17th Century*, 1,590 p. repr. Seaby, 1967.

R. C. Bell, *Copper Commercial Coins, 1811–19*, 238 p. Corbitt & Hunter, 1964.

British Commonwealth

R. P. Harris, *A Guidebook of Modern British Commonwealth Coins*, 123 p. Western Pub. Co., 1970.

J. Remick, S. James, P. Finn and A. Dowle, *British Commonwealth Coins, 1649–1971*, 500 p. Canadian Numismatic Pub. Inst., 1971.

F. Pridmore, *The Coins of the British Commonwealth of Nations, Pts I–III*, 829 p. Spink, 1960–65.

R. Friedburg, *Coins of the British World from AD 500 to the Present*, 210 p. Coin & Currency Inst., 1965.

Europe

J. S. Davenport, *European Crowns, 1700–1800*, 334 p. Spink, 1965.

J. S. Davenport, *European Crowns and Talers since 1800*, 423 p. Spink, 1965.

J-P. Divo, *Modern Greek Coins, 1828–1968*, 100 p. 1969.

F. C. Higgins, *Copper Coins of Europe till 1892*, 95 p. 1970.

Hobson Burton, *Catalogue of Scandinavian Coins*, 128 p. Oak Tree Press, 1970.

R. Kain, *Russische Numismatik*, 256 p.

F. Morin, *Catalogue of Belgian Coins, 1832–1964*, 87 p. 1966.

K. F. Morrison and H. Grunthal, *Carolingian Coins*, 465 p.

A. Pagani, *Monete Italiane, 1796–1963*, 381 p. 2nd ed.

H. M. Severin, *The Silver Coinage of Imperial Russia, 1682–1917*, 276 p. Spink, 1965.

V. G. (Victor Guilloteau), *Monnaies Françaises*, 2 vols, 829 p.

R. P. Harris, *A Guidebook of Modern European Coins*, 202 p. Whitman Pub. Co., 1965.

H. Schlumberger, *Gold Coins of Europe since 1800*, 352 p. Oak Tree Press, 1969.

North and Central America

J. E. Charlton, *Standard Catalogue of Canadian Coins, Tokens and Paper Money*, 200 p. Whitman Pub. Co., 1965.

C. M. Robinson, *The Coins of Central America*, 131 p.

R. S. Yeoman, *A Guidebook of United States Coins*, 254 p. Whitman Pub. Co., 1971.

G. C. Criswell, Jnr, *North American Currency: The Standard Paper Money Reference*

R. Werlich, *Catalogue of U.S., Canadian and Confederate Currency*, 114 p. Quaker Press, 1969.

R. P. Harris, *A Guidebook of Modern Latin Coins*, 125 p. 1966.

N. Shafer, *A Guidebook of Modern U.S. Currency*, 160 p. 3rd ed., Whitman Pub. Co., 1965.

C. Elizondo, *Eight Reales and Pesos of the New World*, 139 p. 1968.

Asia, Africa and the Far East

J. Allen, *Coins of Ancient India*, 318 p. Whitman Pub. Co., 1965.

A. B. Coole, *Coins in China's History*, 159 p. 4th ed., Coole, 1965.

J. S. Davenport, *The Dollars of Africa, Asia and Oceania*, 207 p. 1969.

E. Kann, *Illustrated Catalog of Chinese Coins*, 476 p. repr. 1967.

A. Kaplan, *The Coins of South Africa*, 68 p. 3rd ed., 1965.

K. Oka, *Silver Crowns of the Far East*, 115 p.

F. Schjoth, *Chinese Currency*, 88 p. 2nd ed., 1965.

W. H. Valentine, *Modern Copper Coins of the Muhammadan States*, 203 p. Spink, 1969.

A. E. H. Petrie, *Manchu Mints*,

A. B. Coole, *An Encyclopedia of Chinese Coins*, 581 p. Coole, 1967.

R. L. Clarke, *A Catalog of the Coins of British Oceania*, 77 p. 1964.

Paper Currency

C. Narbeth, *Collecting Paper Money*, 134 p. Lutterworth, 1968.

E. P. Newman, *The Early Paper Money of America*, 360 p. 1966.

R. S. Toy, *World War II Allied Military Currency*, 79 p.

R. S. Toy and B. Meyer, *World War II Axis Military Currency*, 98 p. 1967.

D. M. Miller, *Bank of England and Treasury Notes, 1694–1970*, Corbitt & Hunter, 1970.

INDEX

INDEX

Albums, 43
America, 62, 74, 77, 116–17, 140
Annual percentage increase, 6
Antique shops, 29
Auctions, 33–4, 38–9, 152–3
Australia, 75, 76, 90, 116–17

Bahamas, 56, 57, 75, 76, 90, 131
Banknotes, 139–41
Bermuda, 90
Brass threepence, 19–20, 21–2, 64, 65. *See also* specific monarchs
British Museum, 48, 129
Brockages, 114
Buying, methods of, 29–34, 39

Canada, 69, 72, 75, 76, 91, 117
Catalogues, 5, 25, 31, 33–4, 41, 49, 57, 64, 74, 102, 107
Charles I, 81, 86
Churchill crown, 6, 56, 59, 73, 81, 86–7, 90, 107
Clubs, 37, 47–8, 140
Coin cases, 43
Commonwealth: crown-size coins, 89–93; proof sets, 58. *See also* individual countries
Conditions of coins, 8–9, 10–13, 19–22, 31, 38, 80
Cook, Captain, 72, 92
Coronation issues, 54, 55, 86, 90, 136
Crown, 6, 21, 81–93, 106. *See also* individual monarchs

Dealers, 18, 31–3, 36–7, 38, 48, 59, 130, 151–2
Decimal coins, 61–2
Decimalization, 13, 17, 23, 89

Denominations, 142–50
Diamond Jubilee, 136–7
Die, 10, 15–16, 53, 86, 114, 119–20
Dollar, 81, 115–18, 130
Double-faced coins, 111
Double florin, 87–8

Edward II, 101
Edward VI, 81
Edward VII, 5, 13, 102, 107, 136, 137; crown, 4–5, 84, 88; farthing, 4–5, 95, 97; florin, 4–5; gold coins, 107; halfcrown, 4–5, 63, 108, 125; halfpenny, 4–5; 'low tide' coins, 64, 122; Maundy coins, 102, 104; penny, 5, 64, 66; proof set, 55; shilling, 4–5; silver coins, 108; sixpence, 4–5; threepence, 4–5; third-farthing, 99; type set, 4–5, 60
Edward VIII, 13, 49, 97, 109, 110, 137
Eire, 17, 25, 69, 75, 77
Elizabeth II, 12, 17, 60, 88, 91, 92, 110; crown, 6, 86–7, 88, 90; farthing, 96, 97; gold coins, 108; halfcrown, 65; Maundy coins, 103, 105; penny, 66, 110; proof set, 55; shilling, 15; threepence, 19–20, 65; type set, 59–61, 65

Farthing, 6, 64, 75, 94–7, 110. *See also* individual monarchs
Festival of Britain, 55, 85
Fiji, 57, 91
Five pounds, 107, 108
Florin, 12, 21, 61, 110. *See also* individual monarchs